# A CATECHISM OF MUSIC

Owing to the antiquity and rarity of this book, certain pages are regrettably absent, and readability is compromised due to the blurring of the original text. If you possess any insights regarding the availability of these missing sections, kindly inform us. Your assistance is crucial in ensuring the completion of this significant work for the benefit of future generations.

# A CATECHISM OF MUSIC

J. JOUSSE
&
LOUIS C. ELSON

GYAN

*Published by*

Gyan Publishing House
5, Ansari Road
Daryaganj, New Delhi-110002
Phone: 011-47034999, 9811692060
E-mail: books@gyanbooks.com

*Distribution Network*
gyanbooks.com
India, USA, Canada, UK, Australia



ISBN: 978-93-7225-779-3 (PB)

First Published, 1907

2nd Impression 2025

*Printed at:* Gyan Press, Delhi.



**A CATECHISM OF MUSIC**
Author: J. JOUSSE & LOUIS C. ELSON

CONSERVATORY EDITION

# A Catechism of Music

BY

J. JOUSSE

Revised and Edited by

LOUIS C. ELSON and H. L. HEARTZ

With an Addendum Containing

*An Elementary Treatise on Piano Technique Compiled from the Works of Richter, Marx, Burrowes, etc.*

White-Smith Music Publishing Co.

BOSTON NEW YORK CHICAGO

# CONTENTS



## ADDENDUM

# KEY-BOARD OF A MODERN SEVEN OCTAVE PIANO EXPLAINED

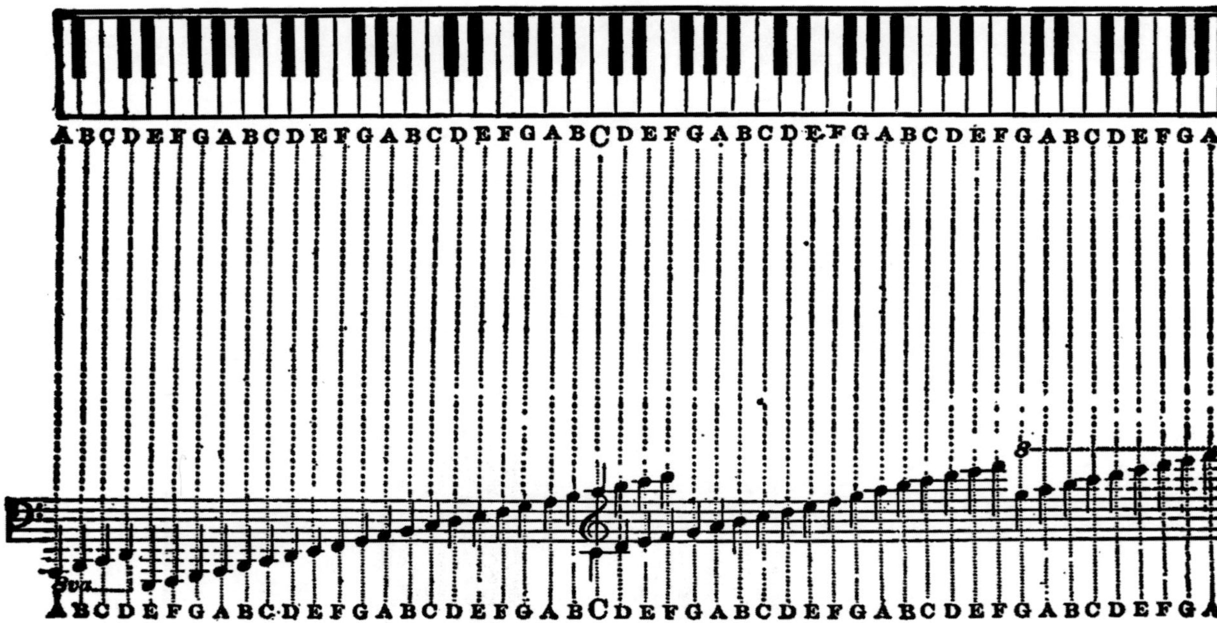


Bass part, usually played by the left hand.

Treble part, usually played by the right hand.

# A CATECHISM OF MUSIC

## SECTION I

### STAFF, NOTES, AND CLEFS

**What is music?**

Music is the art of grouping musical tones in succession or combination.

**What is a tone?**

A sound of definite pitch (high or low), value (long or short), and power (loud or soft).

**What is a succession of musical tones denominated?**

Melody.

**What name is applied to musical tones in combination?**

Harmony.

**How are musical ideas expressed in writing?**

By characters called notes and rests.

**How many notes are used?**

Seven.

**How are they named?**

By the first seven letters of the alphabet — A, B, C, D, E, F, G.*

---

* In Italy and France, the notes are expressed by the following syllables:—

| do, | re, | mi, | fa, | sol, | la, | si. |
|---|---|---|---|---|---|---|
| C, | D, | E, | F, | G, | A, | B. |

How are the notes written?

On five parallel lines and their spaces, which, taken collectively, are termed the *staff.*

LINES SPACES

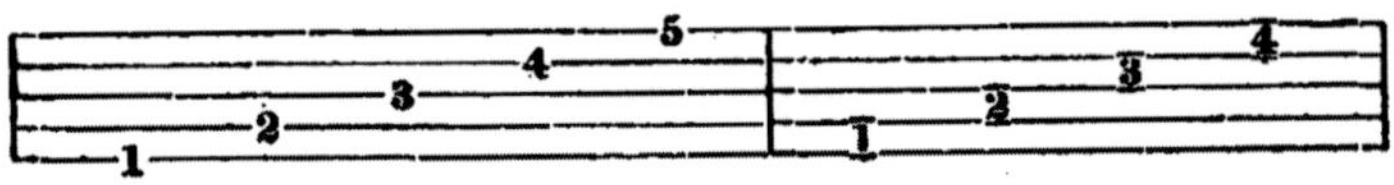


How are the lines and spaces of the staff counted?

From the bottom upwards.

How are the names of the notes and their pitch ascertained?

By means of a character called a *clef,* which is placed at the beginning of the staff.

How many clefs are used in pianoforte music?

Two, viz., the treble clef and the bass clef.

What line of the staff is the treble clef placed upon?

On the second line from the bottom.

What note or letter does it make?

The letter or note G.

TREBLE CLEF.

What are the notes on the five lines of the treble staff?

The first line is E; the second, G; the third, B; the fourth, D; and the fifth. F

**Notes on the Lines.**

**What are the notes in the four spaces?**

The first space is F; the second, A; the third, C; and the fourth, E.

**Notes in the Spaces.**

**Are the notes always confined within the five lines and four spaces of the staff?**

No; they frequently extend above or below; then additional lines, called *leger lines* are added above or below the staff, and the notes are placed on or between them.

**What are the notes on the additional lines above the treble staff?**

The first additional line is A; the second, C; the third, E; the fourth, G; the fifth, B.

**What are the notes in the additional spaces?**

The first space is G; the second, B; the third, D; the fourth, F; the fifth, A; the sixth, C.

**What are the notes on the additional lines below the treble staff?**

The first additional line is C; the second is A.

**What are the notes in the additional spaces below the staff?**

The first space below is D; the second, B; the third, G.

*Names of the Notes on the Treble Staff*

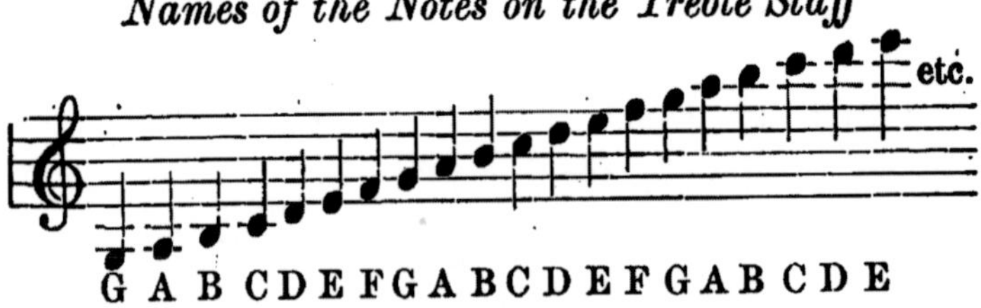


**NOTE.—The notes on the Treble Staff should be acquired before the pupil attempts learning those of the Bass Staff.**

**On what line is the bass clef placed?**

On the fourth line from the bottom.

**What note or letter does it make?**

The note or letter F.

BASS CLEF

F

**What are the notes on the five lines of the bass staff?**

The first line is G; the second line, B; the third line, D; the fourth line, F; and the fifth line, A.

G B D F A

1 2 3 4 5

**What are the notes in the four spaces of the bass staff?**

The first space is A; the second, C; the third, E; and the fourth, G.

1 2 3 4

A C E G

**What are the notes on the additional lines above the bass staff?**

The first line is C; the second, E; the third, G.

C E G

**What are the notes in the additional spaces above the bass staff?**

The first space above is B; the second, D; and the third, F.

B D F

**What are the notes on the additional lines below the bass staff?**

The first line below is E; the second, C; the third, A; and the fourth, F

E C A F

**What are the notes in the additional spaces below the bass staff?**

The first additional space is F; the second, D; the third, B; and the fourth, G.

F D B G

*Names of the Notes on the Bass Staff*

F G A B C D E F G A B C D E F G A B C

## SECTION II

### THE KEY-BOARD, AND NAMES OF KEYS

How many white keys are there on a seven octave pianoforte ?

Fifty.

What are they called ?

Naturals.

How many black keys are there ?

Thirty-five.

What are they called?

Sharps and flats.

On what key is the bass clef note played, reckoning from the bottom ?

On F; two octaves above the lowest F.

On what key is the treble clef note played ?

On G; nine notes above F, the bass clef note.

How are the keys divided ?

The white keys are in regular succession throughout the key-board; the black keys are divided into clusters of three and two alternately.

What is the name of the white key before the two black keys ?

It is called C.

What is the name of the white key before the three black keys ?

It is called F.

Can you by these two keys, C and F, find the name of any other key ?

Yes; by naming the keys according to the order of the seven letters, A, B, C, D, E, F, G.

What is the use of the black keys ?

Each black key serves for the sharp of the note below, and for the flat of the note above. The black key above C is C♯, which black key serves also for D♭.

Where are B sharp and E sharp played, as there is no black key above these notes ?

On the keys of C and F natural.

Where are C flat and F flat played, as there is no black key below these notes ?

On B and E natural.

Why is there no black key between B and C, or between E and F ?

Because these notes are only a semitone distant from each other; the other white keys, being at the distance of a tone from each other, are parted by a black key.

---

## SECTION III

### THE DIFFERENT KINDS OF NOTES AND THEIR PROPORTIONS

How many different kinds of notes are there?

Six.

What are they ?

*The whole, half, quarter, eighth, sixteenth* and *thirty second.*

Describe their shape ?

1. The *whole note* is an open oval, written thus: 𝅝

2. The *half* is an oval with a stem: 

3. The *quarter* is a black dot with a stem: 

4. The *eighth* is a black dot with a stem and a dash attached: 

5. The *sixteenth* has two dashes to its stem: 

6. The *thirty-second* has three dashes to its stem: 

What proportion do these notes bear to each other?

Each note is equal in duration to one half of the preceding note, and double in duration the succeeding note.

### *Proportion of the Notes in Common Time*

1. How many halves make a whole note?

Two.

How many quarters make a whole note?

Four.

How many eighths in a whole note?

Eight.

How many sixteenths in a whole note?

Sixteen.

How many thirty-seconds in a whole note?

Thirty-two.

2. How many quarters in a half note?

Two.

How many eighths in a half note?

Four.

How many sixteenths in a half note?

Eight.

How many thirty-seconds in a half note?

Sixteen.

3. How many eighths make a quarter?

Two.

How many sixteenths?

Four.

How many thirty-seconds?

Eight.

4. How many sixteenths make an eighth?

Two.

How many thirty-seconds in a sixteenth?

Two.

The pupil is advised to write exercises on the proportion of the notes in common and triple time.

---

A whole note 𝅝 is also called a semibreve.

A half note 𝅗𝅥 is also called a minim.

A quarter note 𝅘𝅥 is also called a crotchet.

An eighth note 𝅘𝅥𝅮 is also called a quaver.

A sixteenth note 𝅘𝅥𝅯 is also called a semiquaver.

A thirty-second note 𝅘𝅥𝅰 is also called a demisemiquaver.

TIME-TABLE.

The stems of the notes may be turned up or down, tied or not, without changing the duration of the notes.

---

## SECTION IV

### THE DOT, AND PROPORTION OF NOTES IN TRIPLE TIME

What is the effect of a dot after a note?

It makes the note half as long again.

How many half notes are there in a dotted whole note?

Three.

How many quarter notes in a dotted whole note?

Six.

**How many eighths?**
Twelve.

**How many sixteenths?**
Twenty-four.

**2. How many quarters in a dotted half?**
Three.

**How many eighths?**
Six.

**How many sixteenths?**
Twelve.

A dotted half is equal to 3 or 6 or 12

**3. How many eighths make a dotted quarter?**
Three.

**How many sixteenths?**
Six.

A dotted quarter is equal to 3 or 6

**4. How many sixteenths in a dotted eighth?**
Three.

**How many thirty-seconds?**
Six.

A dotted eighth is equal to 3 or six

**How many thirty-seconds make a dotted sixteenth?**
Three.

## *The Double Dot*

**What is the effect of a double dot after a note?**
It makes the note three-fourths longer.

To what is a double dotted half equal?

A half, quarter and eighth note.

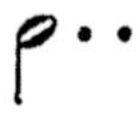 equal to 

To what is a double dotted quarter equal?

A quarter, eighth and sixteenth note.

 equal to 

---

## SECTION V

### RESTS, OR SILENT SIGNS

What are rests?

Signs which denote a silence equal in duration to the respective note they represent.

How is a whole rest expressed?

By a small stroke placed under a line of the staff.

How is a half rest expressed?

By a small stroke over a line

WHOLE REST. HALF REST.

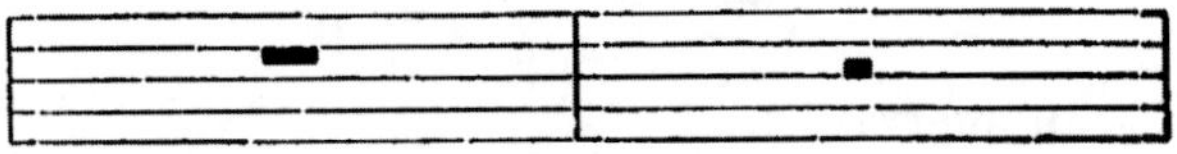

How is a quarter rest represented?

With one of the following signs 𝄽 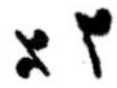

How is an eighth rest represented?

With the following character 𝄾

QUARTER RESTS. EIGHTH REST.

How is sixteenth rest made?

With the following character 𝄿

How is a thirty-second rest made?

With the following character 𝅀

SIXTEENTH REST. THIRTY-SECOND REST.

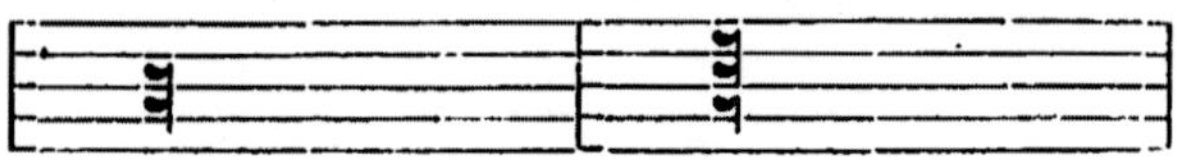

When the duration of a rest is prolonged, how is it expressed?

By placing a dot after the rest.

QUARTER REST DOTTED. EQUAL TO.

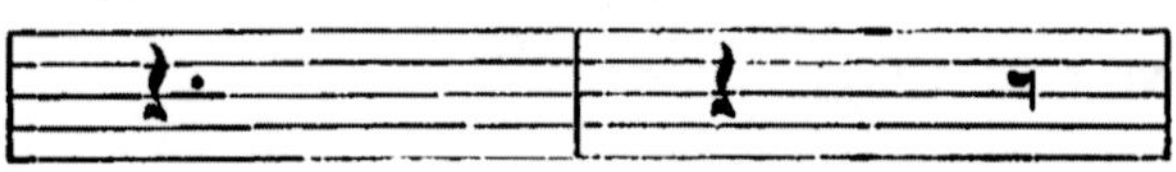

## SECTION VI

### INTERVALS

What is an interval?

The difference of pitch between two tones.

What is pitch?

The height or depth of a musical sound.

What is a semitone?

The smallest interval on the pianoforte; that is, the distance from any note to the next above or below; as B to C, or B to B flat; C to B, or C to C sharp.

**How many kinds of semitones are there?**

Two; diatonic and chromatic.

**What is a diatonic semitone?**

Contiguous notes or keys named by a different letter; as, C to B, C to D flat.

**What is a chromatic semitone?**

Contiguous notes or keys named by the same letter; as, B to B flat, C to C sharp.

**What is a tone?**

The interval comprising two semitones; as from C to D, from C sharp to D sharp, or from C to B flat.

**How are other intervals defined?**

By numbers, counted from any given note, which is always regarded as the first.

**Are intervals reckoned upwards or downwards?**

Upwards, unless the contrary is specified.

**What is the second from C?**

D.

**What is the third from C?**

E.

**What is the fourth from C?**

F.

**What is the fifth from C?**

G.

**What is the sixth from C?**

A.

What is the seventh from C ?

B.

What is the eighth or octave from C ? *

C.

---

## SECTION VII

### THE SHARP, FLAT, AND NATURAL

What is the effect of a sharp (♯) ?

It raises the note before which it is placed a semitone, and this is played on the next key to the right.

F natural. F sharp. C natural. C sharp.

What is the effect of a flat (♭) ?

It lowers the note before which it is placed a semitone, and this is played on the next key to the left.

B natural. B flat. E natural. E flat.

Is it neccessary to mark every sharp or flat required in a composition ?

No; the sharps and flats necessary to the key are marked at the beginning of each line, and constitute the signature. These continue throughout the piece, unless contradicted by naturals.

---

* The teacher should ask the intervals to any other given note; as D, E, F, and the pupil find the answers.

**What is the effect of a natural (♮)?**

It contradicts either the sharp or the flat, and brings the note back to its original state.

F. F sharp. F natural. B. B flat. B natural.

**Are the black keys ever used as naturals?**

No; the naturals are exclusively white keys, although some white keys are used as flats and sharps likewise.

**Which white keys are used as flats and sharps?**

The two white keys having no black note between; which are respectively C flat and B sharp; F flat and E sharp.

**Which is the first sharp?**

F sharp.

**Which is the second sharp?**

C sharp, the fifth note in alphabetical order above F sharp.

1st sharp. 2d sharp.

1 2 3 4 5

**Which is the third sharp?**

G sharp, the fifth note in alphabetical order above C sharp.

2d sharp. 3d sharp.

1 2 3 4 5

Which is the fourth sharp?

The fourth sharp is D sharp; the fifth A; the sixth E; and the seventh B sharp.

Which are the seven sharps when placed according to their order?

The seven sharps are F, C, G, D, A, E, and B.

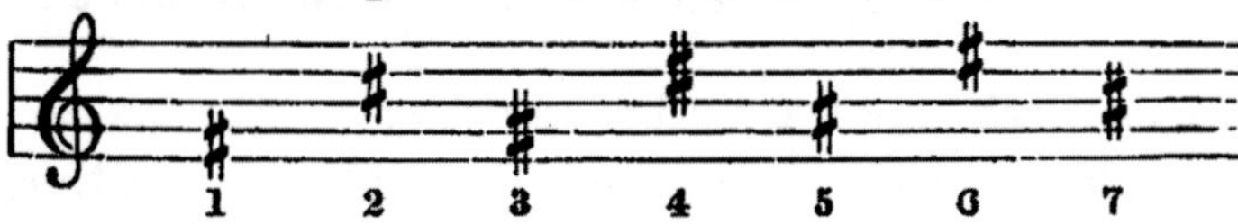


Which is the first flat?

B flat.

Which is the second flat?

The fourth note in alphabetical order above B flat. Thus, the first flat being B, by counting four from that note — B, C, D, E, the second flat will fall on E.

1st flat. 2d flat.

Which is the third flat?

The third flat is A flat.

2d flat. 3d flat.

Which is the fourth flat?

The fourth flat is D flat.

3d flat. 4th flat.

**Which is the fifth flat?**

The fifth flat is G flat; the sixth flat is C flat; and the seventh flat is F flat.

**What is the order of the seven flats?**

The seven flats are B, E, A, D, G, C, and F.

**Is that order always preserved in the signature?**

Yes; the second flat or sharp is never placed after the clef, unless preceded by the first; nor the third without the first and second.

---

## SECTION VIII

### THE DOUBLE SHARP, AND DOUBLE FLAT

**What is the effect of a double sharp?**

A double sharp (×) raises a note already sharp another semitone.

**Which is the note played?**

A note with a double sharp is played two keys higher; therefore F double sharp is played on G.

Same as G.

F natural. F sharp. F double sharp.

**How is the double sharp contradicted?**

By a natural followed by a sharp.

F sharp. F double sharp. F single sharp.

**What is the effect of a double flat?**

A double flat (♭♭) lowers a note already flat another semitone; B double flat is played two keys lower.

Same as A.

B natural. B flat. B double flat.

**How is a double flat contradicted?**

By a natural followed by a flat.

B flat. B double flat. B flat.

---

## SECTION IX

### THE SCALE AND ITS FORMATION

**What is the meaning of the word *scale*?**

This name is given to a succession of seven notes, ascending or descending.

**How many sorts of scales are there in music?**

Two; the *diatonic* and the *chromatic*.

**Of what does the *diatonic scale* consist?**

It consists of five tones and two semitones.

**How are the tones and semitones arranged in the major scale?**

The major scale proceeds by two successive tones, followed by a semitone, then by three successive tones and a semitone; for instance, the scale of C Major proceeds thus: from C to D a tone, from D to E a tone, from E to F a semitone, from F to G a tone, G to A a tone, A to B a tone, B to C a semitone.

**Where are the semitones placed in the foregoing scale?**

The semitones occur between the third and fourth degrees, and between the seventh and eighth degrees.

**Is the descending major scale the same as the ascending scale?**

Yes.

**How are the tones and semitones placed in the minor scale?**

The minor scale proceeds by one tone, followed by a semitone, then by four successive tones and a semitone: for instance, the scale of A minor proceeds thus—from A to B a tone, from B to C a semitone, C to D a tone, from D to E a tone, from E to F sharp a tone, from F sharp to G sharp a tone, from G sharp to A a semitone.

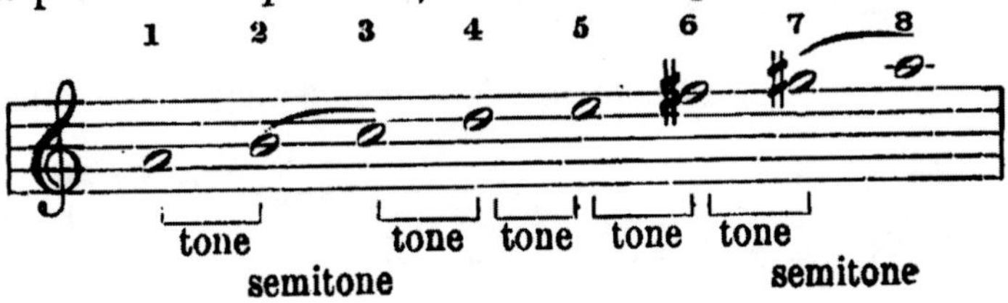

**Where are the semitones placed in the foregoing scale?**

Between the second and third degrees, and between the seventh and eighth.

**How are the tones and semitones placed in the descending minor scale?**

The descending minor scale proceeds by two successive tones and a semitone, then by two other tones and a semitone, and ends by a tone; for instance, the minor scale of A proceeds thus: from A to G a tone, from G to F a tone, from F to E a semitone, from E to D a tone, from D to C a tone, from C to B a semitone, from B to A a tone.

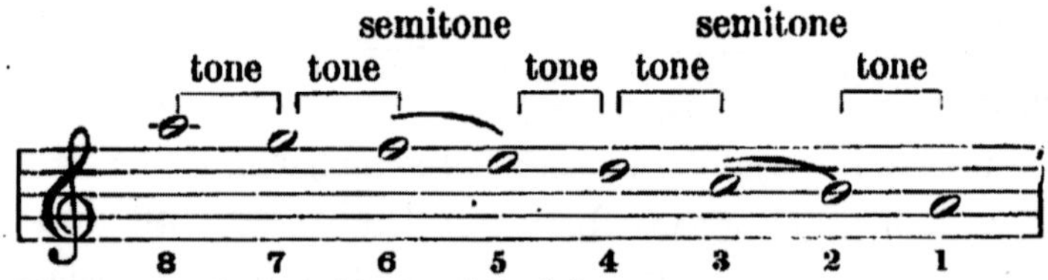


**Where are the semitones placed?**

Between the second and third degrees, and between the fifth and sixth.

## *The Chromatic Scale*

**How is the *chromatic* scale formed?**

It consists of twelve successive semitones, thus: C, D♭, D, E♭, E, F, F♯, G, A♭, A, B♭, B, C.

*Another example, starting on a sharp*

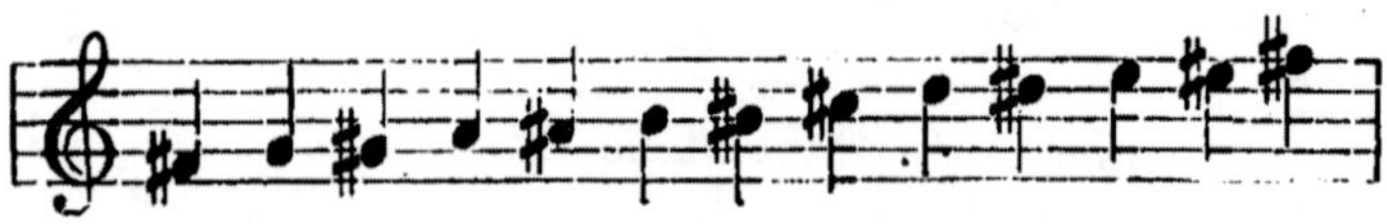

# SECTION X

## THE KEYS AND MODES

**What is the meaning of the word *key*?**

The word *key* implies a regular succession of seven tones, regulated by a principal tone called the *key-note* or *tonic*.

**How many kinds of keys are there?**

Two — major and minor.

**How do you know the major key from the minor?**

The major key is known by its major third, and the minor key by its minor third.

**What is a major third?**

When from the tonic to the third note above there are four semitones (on the pianoforte five keys), the third is *major*, and the key is called a *major* key. C, E, is a major third.

Semitones. Major Third.

**What is a minor third?**

When from the tonic to the third note above there are but three semitones (on the pianoforte four keys), the third is *minor*, and the key a *minor key*.

Semitones. Minor Third.

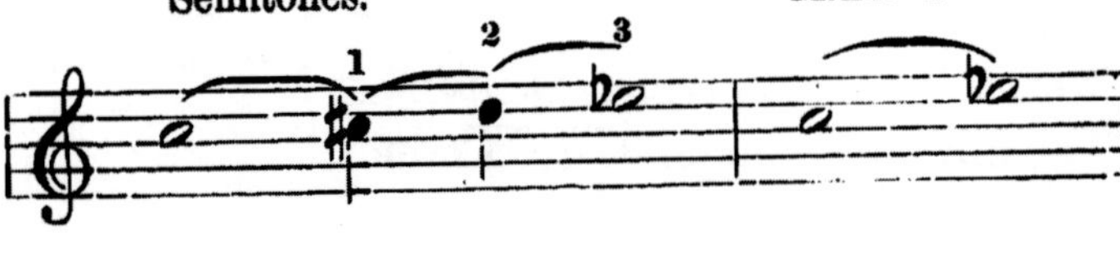

**Are there always two keys, whether you have one, two, three, four, or more sharps or flats at the signature?**

Yes; any key whatever must be either in the major mode and formed like the key of C major, or in the minor mode, and then it is formed like the key of A minor.

**What is the rule respecting the situation of the major and minor keys?**

When sharps are after the clef, the tonic of the major key is the semitone above the last sharp, and the tonic of the minor key is a tone below the last sharp.

**By this rule, what are the keys with one sharp?**

The keys of G major, a semitone above F♯, and E minor, a tone below F♯.

**What are the keys with two sharps?**

The keys of D major and B minor.

**What are the keys with three sharps?**

The keys of A major and F♯ minor.

**What are the keys with four sharps?**

The keys of E major and C♯ minor.

What are the keys with five sharps?

The keys of B major and G♯ minor.

What are the keys with six sharps?

The keys of F♯ major and D♯ minor.

And seven sharps?

C♯ major and A♯ minor.

## *The Keys with Flats at the Signature*

How are the keys with flats situated?

The tonic of the major key is a fifth, and that of the minor key a third above the last flat.

By this rule what are the keys with one flat?

The first flat being B♭, the two keys are F major and D minor; the former a fifth above B♭, and the latter a third above.

What are the keys with two flats?

The second flat being E♭, the two keys are B♭ major and G minor; the former a fifth, and the latter a third above E♭.

**What are the keys with three flats ?**

The third flat being A♭, the two keys are E♭ major and C minor; the former is a fifth, and the latter a third above A♭.

**What are the keys with four flats ?**

The fourth flat being D♭, the two keys are A♭ major and F minor; the first a fifth, and the second a third above D♭.

**What are the keys with five flats ?**

The keys of D♭ major and B♭ minor

**What are the keys with six flats ?**

The keys of G♭ major and E♭ minor.

**And seven flats ?**

C♭ major and A♭ minor.

**How many keys are there ?**

Twelve major and twelve minor keys.

**What are the twelve major keys ?**

*Major Keys*

| | |
|---|---|
| C, no sharp or flat. | F, one flat. |
| G, one sharp. | B♭, two flats. |
| D, two sharps. | E♭, three flats. |
| A, three sharps. | A♭, four flats. |
| E, four sharps. | D♭, five flats. |
| B, five sharps. | G♭, six flats. |

---

**Observe, the keys of B, G♭, and D♭ are used in preference to C♭, F♯ and C♯.**

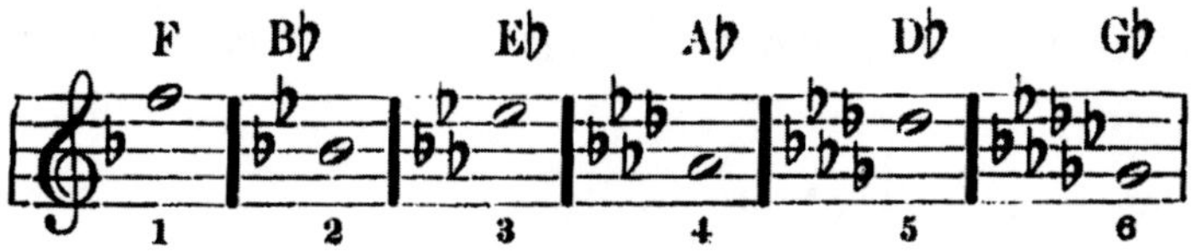


What are the twelve minor keys?

*Minor Keys*

A♮, no sharps or flats.
E, one sharp.
B, two sharps.
F♯, three sharps.
C♯, four sharps.
G♯, five sharps.

D, one flat.
G, two flats.
C, three flats.
F, four flats.
B♭, five flats.
E♭, six flats.

---

**Observe, the keys of B♭ minor and E♭ minor are used in preference to A♯ minor and D♯ minor, and G♯ minor in preference to A♭ minor.**

## SECTION XI

### THE TIME, OR TEMPO

**What is time?**

Time is the measure of sounds with regard to their duration.

**How many kinds of time are there?**

Two principal, viz., *common* and *triple* time.

**How are these two species subdivided?**

Into *simple* and *compound.*

**How is *simple* common time expressed?**

By C, or the same sign with a line through it—₵;* also by $\frac{2}{4}$.

**What must a bar of common time marked C contain?**

Four quarter notes, or the length of a whole note in other notes.

**What does a bar of the other species of common time marked $\frac{2}{4}$ contain?**

It contains either two quarter notes, four eighths, or the length of a half note in each bar.

* Doubling the movement.

**What is the meaning of the figures $\frac{2}{4}$?**

The figure 4 shows that the measure note is a quarter, and the figure 2 indicates that every measure consists of two quarters, or their equivalent in other notes.

**What is compound common time?**

*Compound* common time takes place when two bars of simple triple time are joined into one.

**How many species are there?**

Two principal, viz., $\frac{6}{8}$ and $\frac{12}{8}$ *

**What is the meaning of the figures $\frac{6}{8}$?**

The figure 8 shows that the measure note is an eighth, and the figure 6 indicates that each bar consists of six eighths or their value in other notes.

**What is the meaning of $\frac{12}{8}$?**

That every bar consists of twelve eighths or their value in other notes.

* The other two species, viz., $\frac{6}{4}$ $\frac{12}{4}$, are seldom used in modern music.

## *Triple Time Explained*

**How many sorts of triple time are there?**

Three viz., $\frac{3}{2}$ $\frac{3}{4}$ $\frac{3}{8}$.

**Explain $\frac{3}{2}$.**

The figure 2 shows that the measure note is a half note, and the figure 3 that every bar consists of three half notes or their equivalent.

**Explain the second species $\frac{3}{4}$.**

The figure 4 shows that the measure note is a quarter, and the figure 3, that every bar consists of three quarters.

**Explain the third species $\frac{3}{8}$.**

The figure 8 shows that the measure note is an eighth, and the figure 3, that every bar consists of three eighths.

**How many species of compound triple time are there?**

Two principal, viz., $\frac{9}{8}$ and $\frac{6}{4}$.

**What is the meaning of $\frac{9}{8}$?**

The figures $\frac{9}{8}$ denote that each bar consists of nine eighths, or their value in other notes.

---

## SECTION XII

### COUNTING AND BEATING TIME

**How is the time of a musical composition to be counted?**

Various ways, according to the number of parts contained in each bar; also, according to the speed of the movement.

**In common time marked C how is the time counted?**

The quarter being the measure note, generally four parts are counted in each bar.

However, in a slow movement, it is better to subdivide each part, and to count eight eighth notes in each bar.

How do you count half common time marked $\frac{2}{4}$?
Generally two quarters in a bar.

However, in a slow movement, it is better to count eighths.

How do you count compound common time marked $\frac{6}{8}$?
Generally two dotted quarters in a bar.

However, in a slow movement, it is better to count six eighths.

How do you count triple time marked $\frac{3}{4}$?
Generally three quarters in a bar.

However, in a slow movement, it is better to count six eighths in each bar.

**How do you count triple time marked by the figures $\frac{3}{8}$?**

Three eighths in a bar.

### *Beating Time*

**Is it necessary to beat time?**

Generally speaking, it is better to count it; however, singers and performers on wind instruments being prevented from counting, must beat time.

**What is the manner of beating time?**

By marking with the hand or foot the first part of each bar.

**How is it effected?**

In common time, the hand or foot must fall on the first part of a bar, and rise on the third part.

In triple time, the hand or foot must fall on the first part of the bar, and rise on the third part.

## SECTION XIII

### ITALIAN TERMS OF EXPRESSION RELATING TO TIME AND CHARACTER

**How is the speed of a movement or a piece of music determined?**

Chiefly by the Italian word or words affixed at the beginning.

**What are these words, and what is their meaning?**

The following are some of those in general use; they are classed here from slow to quick.

1. *Grave*, very slow.
2. *Adagio*, a degree faster.
3. *Largo*, slow, and in a large style.
4. *Larghetto*, a degree faster than *largo*.
5. *Andantino*, somewhat slow and flowing.
6. *Andante*, a degree faster than *andantino*.
7. *Moderato*, moderate time.
8. *Allegretto*, lively and tripping.
9. *Allegro*, quick.
10. *Vivace*, quick and vivacious.
11. *Presto*, very quick.
12. *Prestissimo*, as quick as possible.

**What is the meaning of the following words: *assai, molto, più, poco, non troppo*?**

These words, when joined to any of the foregoing, serve to extend or modify their meaning; as

*Adagio non troppo*, not too slow.
*Allegro assai*, somewhat quick.
*Più presto*, quicker than *presto*.
*Poco presto*, almost *presto*.

How is the character of a piece and its style denoted?

Generally by Italian words.

What words are mostly used?

*Affetuoso*, gently.
*Agitato*, with emotion.
*Amoroso*, tenderly.
*Cantabile*, in a singing style.
*Con brio*, with spirit.
*Con fuoco*, with fire.
*Con gusto*, with taste.
*Brillante*, brilliantly.
*Pastorale*, in a simple, unaffected manner.
*Sostenuto*, sustained.
*Scherzando*, playfully.
*Vigoroso*, with vigor.

Where are these words placed?

After the Italian word denoting the speed of the move ment, thus:

*Andante affetuoso.*
*Allegro agitato.*
*Allegro con brio.*
*Andantino amoroso.*

## SECTION XIV

### GRACES, OR EMBELLISHMENTS

**What are the principal graces made use of in musical compositions?**

The *appoggiatura*, the *acciaccatura*, the *turn*, the *trill*, and the *mordent.*

**How is the *appoggiatura* or leaning note (derived from the verb *appoggiare*, to lean) expressed?**

By a small note.

**How many sorts of the *appoggiatura* are there?**

Two, the upper and the lower.

**Explain both.**

The upper *appoggiatura* may be a tone or a semitone above the principal note: the lower one is always a semitone below.

**What is the length of the *appoggiatura?***

It borrows half the value of the large note which it precedes, and which consequently must be played one half shorter.

Written.

Played.

How is the *acciaccatura* expressed and performed?

The *acciaccatura* is also expressed by a small note; but it has a line drawn through it. It is played very short, as its name—derived from the verb *acciaccare*, to crush -- indicates.

Written.

Played.

Explain the *turn*?

The *turn* is the union of the upper and lower *appoggiatura;* it is either direct or inverted.

How is the *direct term* performed?

The *direct turn* begins with the tone or semitone above the principal note; it is marked thus: ∾

Written. Played.

How is the turn to a dotted note played?

The note is played first, and then the turn.

Written. Played.

**How is the *inverted turn* played?**

The *inverted turn* begins with the note below, and ends on the principal note.

Written. Played.

**What is indicated by a sharp, flat, or natural placed over or under a turn?**

A sharp, flat, or natural placed *over* a turn shows that its highest note is to be played sharp, flat, or natural as the case may be; and if *under*, that its lowest note is to be similarly treated.

Written. Played. Written. Played.

**How is the *trill* marked and performed?**

The *trill*, marked by (*tr.*) an abbreviation of the Italian word *trillo*, is a quick and alternate repetition of two notes, the principal note, and the note above.

**How many sorts of *trills* are there?**

Three; the *passing trill*, the *plain trill*, and the *trill* with a turn.

**How are these *trills* performed?**

1. The *passing trill* is very short.

Written. Played.

2. The *plain trill* is longer, but is not ended by a turn.

Written. Played.

3. The *trill with a turn*, which is generally introduced at the end of a piece, is played thus:

Written. Played.

**How is the mordent written and performed?**

The mordent (from Fr., mordre, to bite), is a very short trill, generally consisting of three (but may have five) notes without a turn, and with an accent on the last. It begins and ends on the principal note.

The trill always occupies the full value of the principal note, whereas the last note of the mordent is always much longer than the preceding notes.

Written. Played. Written. Played. Written. Played.

Written. Played. Written. Played.

## SECTION XV

### EXPRESSION

**What are the principal means of expression?**

Strict attention to the accents, emphasis, syncopation, and a close observance of *legato*, *staccato*, *crescendo* and *diminuendo.*

#### 1. *Accents*

**What is meant by *accent* in music?**

The stress given to one note in preference to another, according to its place in the bar or measure.

**Where are the accents placed in common time?**

In common time of four quarter notes in a bar, the first and third part of the *measure* are *accented*, the second and fourth parts *unaccented.*

**Is this order always preserved?**

No; In slow movements, when quarters are divided into eighths, the accents are more frequent; they fall upon the first, third, fifth, and seventh eighths; the second, fourth, sixth, and eighth notes are unaccented.

How are the accents placed in $\frac{2}{4}$?

The first quarter is *accented*, and the others *unaccented.*

How are the accents placed in compound common time, for instance in $\frac{6}{8}$?

When two dotted quarters are introduced, both are *accented*; but the first is most *accented* when six eighths are used, the first and fourth are *accented*, and the others *unaccented.*

ac. un. ac. un. ac. un. ac.

How are the accents placed in triple time?

The first part of the bar is *accented*, the second and third parts *unaccented.*

ac. un. un. ac. un. un. ac. un. un.

In a slow movement, when each bar consists of six eighths, the first, third, and fifth eighths are *accented;* the second, fourth, and sixth are *unaccented.*

Does every piece of music always begin with the first part of the bar?

No; for the sake of keeping the accents in the proper places a piece frequently begins with the last part of the bar; then the last bar of the piece or strain must be short of that part.

(See examples on pages 40 and 42.)

### 2. *Emphasis*

What is meant by emphasis?

*Emphasis* is a deviation from the rules given concerning the accents; it takes place when a note which should not be accented has a stress given to it: for instance, in common time, the second and fourth parts of the bar are unaccented; should a stress be laid on one of these parts, it would be termed an *emphasis.*

How is the emphasis marked?

By a small angle > under or over the note, also by the words *sforzando*, *sforzato*, or their abbreviations *sforz.*, *sf.*

### 3. *Syncopation*

What is the meaning of syncopation?

*Syncopation* takes place when the unaccented part of a bar is joined with the next accented part: this happens —

1. When long notes are placed between two other notes of a shorter duration, as a half note between two quarter notes, or three quarters between two eighths.

OR

2. When two notes are connected by a tie, either in the middle of a bar, or from the last note of a bar to the first of the next.

When syncopation takes place, how can the pianoforte player keep time?

The treble and bass seldom syncopate together; one part generally marks the time by equal notes. But should they go together, the pianist then should count while the syncopated note is sustained.

### 4. *Legato and Staccato*

What is the meaning of the word *legato?*

This Italian word signifies a smooth and connected style of playing, blending the sound of one note with that of the next.

How is this effected?

By keeping each note down until its successor is struck.

How is the *legato* expressed?

By curved lines placed over the notes, these curved lines are termed *slurs.*

What do small dashes placed over notes signify?

That the notes are to be played short and distinct, lifting the finger from the key when one fourth of the length of the note has expired.

Written. Played.

How is that style of playing denominated?

It is called *staccato*, and produces a fine effect when properly contrasted with the *legato* style.

When round dots are placed over the notes, are they played in the same style?

The notes must not be played quite so short: they should have one half of their usual length.

Written. Played.

What is meant when a slur is placed over a succession of dots?

That the finger should be kept down still longer,—the notes having three fourths of their usual length.

Written. Played.

### 5. *Modification of Sounds*.

What is the meaning of the word *piano*, or its abbreviation *pia.* or *p.*, placed under or over some notes?

This Italian word signifies that the notes must be played in a soft and delicate manner.

What is the meaning of *pianissimo*, oftentimes abbreviated *pp.*?

This word is the superlative of *piano*, and denotes the utmost degree of softness in playing.

**What is the meaning of *forte*, mostly abbreviated *f*?**

It indicates that the notes must be played in a loud and forcible manner.

**What signifies *mezzo forte*, or its abbreviation *mf*?**

It indicates the medium between *forte* and *piano*.

**What signifies *fortissimo*, or its abbreviation *ff*?**

This word—the superlative of *f*—shows that the greatest degree of force and pressure of the fingers must be used; avoiding, however, any roughness.

**What is the meaning of the word *crescendo*, or its abbreviation *cresc.*?**

It signifies that the sound must be gradually increased from soft to loud; this is sometimes expressed by an acute angle pointing to the left <.

**What is the meaning of the word *diminuendo*, or its abbreviation *dim.*?**

It signifies that the sound must be gradually diminished from loud to soft: it is sometimes expressed by an acute angle pointing to the right hand >.

**When these two angles are opposite each other, thus < >, what does it imply?**

That the sounds must be gradually increased from soft to loud, and afterwards gradually diminished from loud to soft.

### 6. *Other Marks of Expression*

**What is the meaning of the word *tremando* written over some chords ?**

This Italian word indicates that the chords must be divided into two parts, and played with rapidity like a *trill.*

*Tremando.*

Written. Played.

**What is the meaning of the Italian word *arpeggio* ?**

It signifies that the notes of a chord must be played in rapid succession from the lowest to the highest, instead of striking them all at once. This is sometimes expressed by a waved line placed by the side of the chord.

Written. Played.

**What signifies the word *pedal*, or its abbreviation *ped.* written under a passage ?**

It shows that the loud or right hand pedal must be pressed with the foot, to raise the dampers and let the vibration of the strings continue. A star (*) is usually placed when it is to be discontinued.

**In what passages is the loud pedal introduced ?**

Chiefly in slow passages in which the same harmony

is continued; when the chords are changed, the pedal must be dropped.

What is the meaning of the words *una corda* under a passage?

They indicate the use of the soft pedal—that to the left—which is raised again at the words *tre corde*.

What is the *tie*?

The *tie* is a curved line placed over two notes on the same line or space of the staff.

What is the effect of the *tie*?

The first note only must be struck, and kept down the whole length of the two.

What is a hold?

A hold, marked thus 𝄐, or thus 𝄑, signifies that the note or rest over or under which it is placed is to be prolonged beyond its ordinary value.

When the hold is over the double bar, what is its signification?

When placed over the double bar, the hold shows the end of a strain

## SECTION XVI

### CHARACTERS IN COMMON USE

**What is the use of single lines drawn across the staff ?**

These small lines are called *bars*, and serve to divide a piece of music into equal portions, termed *measures*.

1st strain. 2d strain.

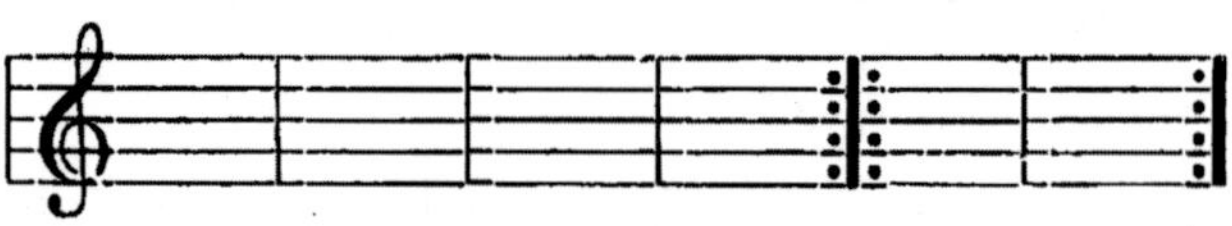

**What is the use of the double bar ?**

It serves to divide a piece of music into two, three, or more parts, called *strains*. When dots are placed on both sides of the double bar, both parts are to be repeated; when the dots are only on one side of the double bar, the part on the same side as the dots is to be repeated.

**What is the use of the *brace* ?** {

It serves in pianoforte music to connect the two staves, the upper of which is for the right hand, and the lower for the left hand.

**What is the meaning of the words *da capo*, or their abbreviation D. C. ?**

They signify that the performer must play over again the first part of a piece from the beginning to the double bar.

**What is the meaning of the words *dal segno?***

These words refer to a preceding mark of *repeat*, and indicate that part of the piece must be repeated from the sign 𝄋, to the double bar.

**What is the use of the figures 1 and 2 placed over some notes at a double bar ?**

They signify that a part of the piece must be played twice over; and that, in playing it the second time, the performer must omit the measure or measures marked 1, and instead play those marked 2.

**What is the meaning of the word *ottava*, generally abbreviated *8va.* followed by dots ?**

This Italian word signifies that the notes, over or under which it is placed, are to be played, respectively, an octave higher or lower.

Written. Played.

Written. Played.

What is the meaning of the word *loco*?

It is generally used after the word *ottava*, and signifies that the music must be played as written. The word *loco*, however, is rarely used in modern music, the termination of the dots serving the same purpose.

What signify the letters R. H. or M. D. under some notes in the bass part?

They signify that these notes are to be played with the right hand — *main droit*, crossing over the left hand.

What signify the letters L. H. or M. G. placed over notes on the treble staff?

That these notes must be played in the treble with the left hand — *main gauche*, crossing over the right hand.*

---

## SECTION XVII

### ABBREVIATIONS AND LICENSES

What is the meaning of a heavy stroke over or under a whole note, or through the stem of a half or quarter note?

It signifies that the note is to be divided into eighths.

Written.

Played.

*Italian, M. D. *mano dritta*, right hand; M. S. *mano sinistra*, L. H.

**What is the meaning of a double or treble stroke through the stem of a half or quarter note?**

It signifies that the half or quarter note is to be divided into sixteenths, or thirty-seconds.

Written. Played.

**What is the meaning of a stroke after a group of notes?**

It signifies that the group is to be repeated.

Written. Played.

### *Licenses*

**What is the meaning of the figure 3 placed over or under three quarter, eighth, or sixteenth notes?**

It signifies that the three quarter, eighth or sixteenth notes, must be played in the time of two; each group is termed a *triplet.*

**What is the meaning of the figure 6 placed over or under six, eighths, or sixteenths ?**

It signifies that the six eighths or sixteenths must be played in the time of four of the same species.*

**Is the same rule observed with respect to other figures, as 5, 7, 9, etc. ?**

Yes; five eighths are played as four, seven as six, and nine as eight, of the same species.

---

## SECTION XVIII

### POSITION AT THE PIANOFORTE

**What is the proper position of the body and arms at the pianoforte ?**

The performer's position, being seated opposite the centre of the keyboard, must be erect, without the appearance of constraint; the arms, from the elbows upwards, must be a little advanced, and close to the body, except when the right hand plays on the upper part, or the left hand on the lower part of the instrument; in which case, the arms are necessarily a little

* The figures 3 or 6 are often omitted; then the manner of grouping the notes indicates the mode of playing them.

extended; the shoulders must never be raised; therefore the seat of the performer must be so adjusted as not to require their elevation.

**What is the proper position of the hands and fingers on the keyboard?**

The hands must be a little above the keys, and turned slightly outward, so as to prevent the thumb from being withdrawn from the keys. The fingers must be somewhat bent; each finger must be over the centre of its respective key; in pressing down a key with the finger, the other must not move, and the finger which has struck a key must be kept down until the next note is played, when it must be raised. When rests occur, the hands must be raised from the keys.

---

## SECTION XIX

### FINGERING

**What is understood by fingering?**

A proper disposition of the fingers in playing a piece of music on the pianoforte. The hands should be kept as much as possible over five keys, so that each finger may cover its respective key, and the motion be scarcely perceived.

**How is the fingering expressed?**

The thumb and four fingers are marked by the figures 1, 2, 3, 4, 5.

When a diatonic succession extends beyond five notes, how is it played?

By passing the thumb under the long fingers in ascending, and these over the thumb in descending.

Under which finger is the thumb to be passed in ascending?

In ascending, the thumb of the right hand may pass under the 2d, 3d, or 4th finger, but not under the little finger.

In descending, the 2d, 3d, or 4th finger may be passed over the thumb, but not the 5th finger.

Is it allowable to pass one of the fingers over another?

No; for, besides being awkward, it would prevent the tones blending.

Is it allowable to play two or three consecutive notes with the same finger?

No; unless a rest intervenes, every note should be played with a different finger.

Which are the principal means of facilitating the execution of rapid passages?

First, by changing fingers when a note is repeated:

Secondly, by making use of contractions:

Thirdly, by extensions.

Which is the proper fingering of the scales?

In the key of C, and in keys with sharps in the signature, viz., G, D, A, E, and B (major and minor), the thumb of the right hand is placed on the first note of the scale, and on the fourth degree, in ascending and descending.

The key of F♯ is an exception to this rule; it is fingered in the following manner:

F♯ Major.

**What is the fingering of the keys with flats in the signature?**

In the major keys of F, B♭, E♭, A♭, and D♭, the thumb of the right hand must be placed on C and F in ascending and descending.

**How are the scales fingered with the left hand?**

In C, and in keys with sharps, the thumb must be placed on the 1st and 5th degrees in the descending and ascending, in major and minor.

The key of B and F♯ form exceptions to this rule; the thumb is placed on the fourth note in ascending, or fifth note in descending.

B Major. F♯ Major.

**How are the scales with flats fingered with the left hand?**

In major keys with flats, as B♭, E♭, A♭, and D♭, the thumb of the left hand must be on the third and seventh degrees of the scale in ascending and descending.

B♭ Major. E♭ Major.

The scale of F, major and minor, is, however, an exception to this rule; it is fingered with the thumb on the first and fifth degrees.

**How are the minor scales with flats fingered with the left hand?**

The minor scales of B♭, E♭, A♭, and D♭, are not fingered as the major scales of the same name: the thumb of the left hand is placed on F and C, in descending and ascending.

B♭ Minor. E♭ Minor.

**What is the best mode of fingering the *chromatic* scale?**

Third finger on *all* the black keys; second finger on F and C in the right, and on E and B in the left hand; thumb on all the other white keys.

Right Hand.

Left Hand.

**NOTE.—Daily exercises on all the scales are strongly recommended to students.**

## SECTION XX

### TRANSPOSITION

**What is meant by *transposition?***

Changing the key of a composition.

The following example, in the first instance in A minor, is transposed to the keys of B and G minor respectively.

*Original Key, A Minor*

*Transposed a whole tone higher, to B Minor*

etc.

*Transposed a whole tone lower, to G Minor*

etc.

**What is necessary to a student to be conversant with *transposition?***

Acquaintance with all clefs and keys.

**Is there any other clef besides the two explained on pages 2 and 5?**

Yes; a third clef, called the C clef, is used in vocal music and in scores.

On what line of the staff is it placed?

It may be placed upon the first, second, third, or fourth lines of the staff; and, according to its situation, indicates a different part.

When placed on the first line, what is it called?

The *canto* or *soprano* clef. This part is sung by female voices of high compass.

C D E F G A B C D E

When placed on the second line, what is it called?

The *mezzo soprano* clef, a part sung by female voices of a medium compass; this clef is not used in modern music.

When placed on the third line, what is the C clef called?

The *alto* or *counter tenor* clef. This part is sung by female voices of very low pitch, or by male voices of high compass.

C D E F G A G F E D C B A

This clef is also used for the *viola* or tenor-violin.

When placed on the fourth line, what is the C clef called?

The *tenor clef*. This part is sung by male voices.

C D E F G F E D C B A G F E

**Are the names of the notes on the lines and spaces the same in every clef?**

No; when the position of the clef is changed, the names of the notes are also changed, as may be seen by the foregoing examples

**How do you transpose from the *soprano* clef to the *treble?***

By reading and playing every note a third lower.

C D E F. G A Read and played.

Written.

**How do you transpose from the *alto* to the *treble* clef?**

By reading every note a degree higher and playing the notes an octave lower.

C D E F G A Read.

Written. Played.

**How do you transpose from the *tenor* to the *bass* clef?**

By reading the notes four degrees lower, and playing them an octave higher.

C D E F E D Played an octave higher.

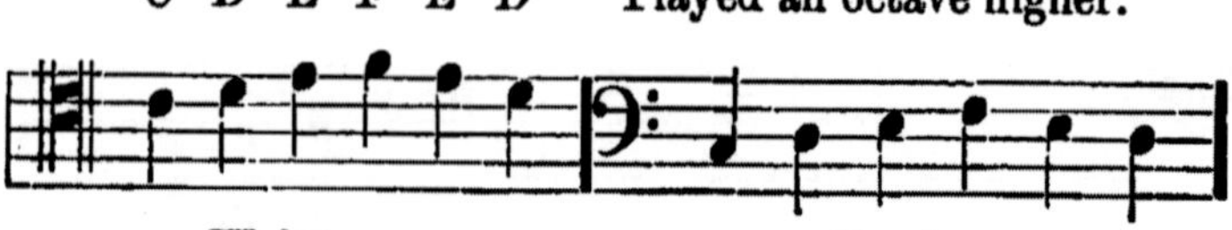

Written. Read.

**Can you transpose from one key to another by means of the different clefs?**

Yes; the following example shows that the same spaces and lines on the staff may be made to represent so many different keys by changing the clefs.

AMERICA, IN THE KEY OF C

*Transposed* into the key of D by the use of the *alto* clef:

*Transposed* into the key of B by the use of the *tenor* clef:

*Transposed* into the key of A by the use of the *soprano* clef:

*Transposed* into the key of E by the use of the *bass* clef:

The student, who by constant application has made himself master of the various points explained in this Catechism, should not rest satisfied with this first step; but by unremitting attention, endeavor to advance still further in the science. Music requires much study and practice before great proficiency can be obtained; and—

"Those who think they have done much, see but little to do."—*Dr. Johnson.*

# ADDENDUM

## SECTION I

### THE KEYBOARD AND INTERVALS

**How are the various octaves on the pianoforte named?**

The deepest *tones* on the pianoforte, beginning at c, up to the next c, are called the

*Countertones;*

the next octave is called the

*Great Octave;*

then follows the

*Small Octave;*

after which follows the

*One Line Octave, Two, Three, Four Line Octave;*

Higher octaves require additional lines.

**Are the deepest notes the same on all instruments?**

No; the deepest string on the Violoncello gives **c** in the great octave, or the *great* C. The deepest string on the tenor is the c in the small octave, or the *small* **c**, and the deepest string on the violin, the small **g**, and so forth.

**How can we signify a Key in writing?**

In writing, great Roman characters are used for the great octave, and small for the small octave—small with one line above or below for the one lined octave—small with two lines above or below for the two lined octave, etc. The whole succession of names of *tones* from the Counter B, is therefore as follows:

Counter B,—C, D, E, F, G, A, B,—c, d, e, f, g, a, b, —$\underline{c}$, $\underline{d}$, $\underline{e}$, $\underline{f}$, $\underline{g}$, $\underline{a}$, $\underline{b}$,—$\underline{\underline{c}}$, $\underline{\underline{d}}$, $\underline{\underline{e}}$, etc.

**How is the key-board divided?**

The counter-tones, the great and small octaves, and at all events a part of the one lined octave, are comprehended under the name of the

*Bass,*

or bass tones. The higher octaves, with the whole of the one-lined octaves, and the higher tones of the small octave, are included under the name of

*Treble,*

or treble tones. The exact boundary would therefore be the one lined c, but it is allowable not to adhere rigidly to that limitation. The whole distribution is but superficial for the sake of despatch when no precise object is in question.

**By what names can we most surely fix these keys and their notation in our memory?**

This is not to be obtained by learning by rote, nor by the note table introduced by some professors; but by a clear insight into the notation and its agreement or coincidence with the tonal system. It must be felt that the *scale of notes is the true image of the scale of sounds*, this latter being the scale properly so called — that the notes ascend and descend by degrees on the lines and spaces, in like manner as do the tones in the scale. Now, the first exercise is to fix any tone or clef — for example, the G clef (the one lined g on the second line) — and from that point to *write* and *name*, upward and downward, the following gradation of notes, viz.:

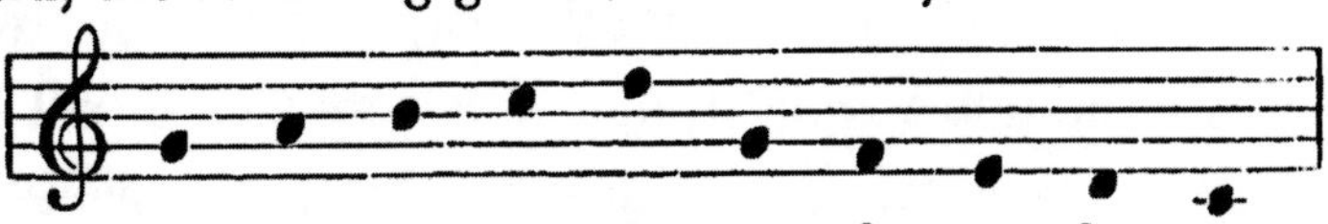

g, a, b, c, d, g, f, e, d, c, etc.

Now let it be observed, that from line to line and space to space, a third *tone* is noted; and let this succession of notes be written upward and downward as follows:

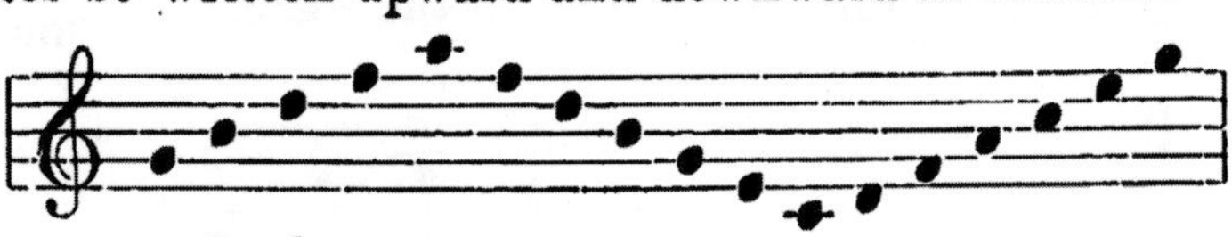

g, b, d, etc.

It will be observed also that upon every third line and every third space, a fifth *tone* is noted, viz.:

e, b, f, c, etc.

Then make a combination of all these enumerated, first one and then the other, thus:

g, e, b, c, e, b, f, d, b,

f, g, b, e, a, b, d, a, c, d

Lastly, take a good musical composition, and read aloud all the notes from it, and if a note should not be immediately recognized, its name can be soon discovered by ascending or descending, degree by degree, to its next neighboring note.

**What is meant by a degree in music ?**

The place occupied by a tone in the scale.

1 degree, 2 d, 3 d, 4 d, 5 d, 6 d, 7 d, 8 d, 9 d, 10 d.

**How are these degrees named ?**

1. Degree or tonic.
2. Degree or super-tonic.
3. Degree or mediant.
4. Degree or sub-dominant
5. Degree or dominant.
6. Degree or sub-mediant.
7. Degree or leading tone (sub-tonic).

The Latin numerals are also used, as.

| | | | |
|---|---|---|---|
| 1st or | Prima. | 8th or | Octave. |
| 2d | Secunda. | 9th | Nona. |
| 3d | Tertia. | 10th | Decima. |
| 4th | Quartia. | 11th | Undecima. |
| 5th | Quinta. | 12th | Duodecima. |
| 6th | Sexta. | 13th | Decimatertia. |
| 7th | Septima. | 14th | Decimaquartia. |

**Are the degrees always counted upwards?**

Usually; but if we wish to designate the contrary we say *Under terza* or *mediant*, or third below; *Under quinta* or *dominant*, or fifth below, etc.

**What is an interval?**

An interval is the difference in pitch between two tones. It must be remembered that all intervals are called according to the degrees of the staff, or according to the numbers of letters they are distant from each other.

For instance, Fig. 1 is a Second; Fig. 2 a Sharp Second; but if the same keys are struck, and called (Fig. 3), the interval is that called a third:

Fig. 1 Fig. 2 Fig. 3

**Are intervals to be reckoned downwards?**

Always upwards from the note named, unless the contrary be expressed.

**What is a tone?**

It consists of two semitones. The interval between F and F sharp is one semitone, and between F sharp and G is another. For example,

consequently the interval between F and G is a whole tone.

**What is a minor or lesser third?**

A minor third (sometimes improperly called a flat third) is three semitones from the note named. For example, the Minor Third of A must be reckoned thus: from A to A sharp *one* semitone, to B *two*, to C *three*.

**How many semitones is a Major or Greater Third from the note named?**

Four; (this interval is sometimes improperly called a sharp third).

**As the semitone above C may be called either C sharp or D flat, is it immaterial in reckoning the Major Third of A whether you say C sharp or D flat?**

No; the Major Third of A must be called C sharp. For example: A, B, C, is a third; and A, B, C, D, is a fourth.

**Name, write, or play Minor and Major Thirds to A, B, C, D, E, F, G; to A♯, B♯, C♯, D♯, E♯, F♯, G♯; to A♭, B♭, C♭, D♭, E♭, F♭, G♭.**

**How many semitones is a perfect fifth from the note named?**

Seven;

but the easiest way is to remember, that every note excepting one has a fifth, either sharp, flat, or natural, like itself. For example, the fifth of C is G, the fifth of C sharp is G sharp, the fifth of C flat is G flat.

**What note has a fifth unlike itself?**

B; the fifth of which must be raised a semitone to make it perfect. For example, the fifth of B is F sharp, the fifth of B sharp is F double sharp, the fifth of B flat is F.

**Name or write fifths to all the notes, beginning with F and proceeding always a fifth higher?**

F, C, G, D, A, E, B, F♯, C♯, D♯, A♯, E♯, B♯. F×, C×, etc.

**Name fifths to flats now commencing with F flat.**

F♭, C♭, G♭, D♭, A♭, E♭, B♭, F♮, etc.

**By way of exercise, now name the fifths below, and observe that in reckoning downwards every note has a fifth like itself excepting F, the fifth below which must be lowered a semitone; for example, the fifth below F flat is B double flat. the fifth below F sharp is B.**

B, E, A, D, G, C, F, B♭, E♭, A♭, D♭, G♭, C♭, F♭, B♭♭, etc.

Name the fifths below to the sharps, commencing with B sharp.

B♯, E♯, A♯, D♯, G♯, C♯, F♯, B♮, etc.

Name again the two letters which have fifths not sharp, flat, or natural, like themselves.

B, in reckoning fifths upward, and F, in fifths downward.

What is the leading note?

The leading note is the sharp Seventh of the scale; it is eleven semitones from the note named; but the easiest way is to reckon it one semitone below the octave:

As you say sharp Seventh, is the leading note always a sharp?

No; for example, the leading note of F is E natural, the leading note of A is G sharp, and the leading note of C flat is B flat.

As the leading note is one semitone below the octave, is it immaterial whether the leading note A be called G sharp or A flat?

No; for although A flat is a semitone below the octave, it is the eighth letter or degree, and the leading note must be the seventh.

Name or write the leading note of A; of B, C, D, E, F, G; of A♯, B♯, C♯, D♯, E♯, F♯, G♯; A♭, B♭, C♭, D♭, E♭, F♭, G♭.

Name or write Minor Thirds, Major Thirds, Fifths, and leading notes to A, B, C, D, E, F, G; A♯, B♯, C♯, D♯, E♯, F♯, G♯; A♭, B♭, C♭, D♭, E♭, F♭, G♭.

**Name or write Minor Thirds, Major Thirds, Fifths, and leading notes to A♭, B♯, C, D♭, E♯, F, G♭ ; A♯, B, C♭, D♯, E, F♭, G♯, A, B♭, C♯, D, E♭, F♯, G.**

---

## SECTION II

### ACCENT AND SYNCOPATION

**What is syncopation ?**

First: an obliteration of the accented notes, by binding them together with the unaccented, and in such a manner that the unaccented note alone is struck, without the accent falling on it. Such a syncopation may occur in all kinds of notes, parts, and members of bars.

Syncopation with parts of bars:

Syncopation with members of bars:

Secondly: placing the accent on notes that were originally unaccented:

Thirdly: when, in simple or compound triple time, the second and third beats in the bar (unaccented notes) are united in one, and an extra stress is thus laid on the second beat:

**But does the third example really merit the title of syncopation?**

In the strictest sense it does not; although resembling syncopation it does not obliterate any former real accent. This resemblance may be in part removed by playing the first beat in the bar *forte:*

On the other hand it may be increased by strengthening the second note:

By this means we may produce a kind of syncopation in common time, thus:

By these various means we may alter the feeling of accent, but not that of measure. But there are also kinds of syncopation in which the time appears so altered that we fancy a new kind is suddenly introduced:

Here for instance, it sounds as though the $\frac{3}{4}$ bar was changed into one of $\frac{3}{4} - \frac{4}{4}$.

**What is an initial imperfect bar?**

The imperfect bar that commences a piece:

What is wanting in the first bar must be given in the last, and what the first has must be deducted from the last bar in a part, so that the two portions may form one perfect bar, thus:

## SECTION III

### ADDITIONAL EMBELLISHMENTS

What is a double trill?

A trill on two notes at once.

What is a chain of trills?

A succession of trills on several successive notes.

If the trill commences with the principal note, as at 1, the turn after each note is effective; if the trill begins from the note above, a turn may be made after each one, but it is better not to introduce the turn until the last, as at 2.

What is the usual term for these groups of notes?

They are termed grace notes.

Why are they not written exactly as they are to be played?

Because too many notes and too much space would be required; this is avoided by the sign of abbreviation. This is especially the case with the trill; but where the signs require as much time to write down as would the notes themselves, it is better to write the latter at once. This has not become generally customary, although our modern composers begin to choose the latter-mentioned manner of writing.

---

## SECTION IV

### ORDINARY FORMS OF COMPOSITION

What is a sonata?

A composition for an instrument of three or four movements, each differing in character, yet bearing a general resemblance to each other. The first movement is usually an allegro. Sometimes this is preceded by an introduction (adagio or andante). The second movement becomes an adagio, andante, or theme with variations, and so on. The third movement is a minuet or scherzo, with trio, and the last a finale, in the manner of the first movement, or a rondo. Many sonatas have no minuet or scherzo, and consist of three movements alone. There are other exceptions, all of which are easily recognizable. Duos, trios, quartuos, etc., all possess this form, as we have already remarked in speaking of the quartette form.

What is a sonatina?

A sonata of small dimensions and lighter character, consisting of two, or at most three, movements.

What is an overture?

An orchestral piece consisting of one great movement, which usually progresses in one tempo — allegro — and without signs of repetition. The overture sometimes has an introduction, however. Its correct form is that of the first movement of a sonata, but, as we have already remarked, without signs of repetition.

What is a symphony?

An orchestral composition in the large sonata form. Its movements, as well as those of all instrumental works hitherto named, are constructed in the same manner as those of the quartette which we have described.

What is a concerto?

A composition for one or several instruments, in which the solo performers display technical facility and taste, while the orchestra merely accompanies. It consists of three movements, an allegro, an adagio, and a finale or rondo. The allegro begins with a tutti, then the performer enters with his first solo, then comes a second tutti, followed by a second solo, then a third tutti and a third solo, and a short tutti closes the movement. The last movement has the same form. The adagio or andante is in the form of a sonata. In later times these three movements have been much shortened, concentrated in one large movement, and the smaller form is now called a concertino.

What is a fantasia?

A composition the form of which is left to the taste and fancy of the composer. It has its periods, groups, and parts, like other compositions, but the arrangement, and combination of these are ordered in so many and various ways that, while we may analyze the form of each separate fantasia, we cannot describe that of the fantasia in general in such a manner as to explain the form of all.

What is a caprice?

A composition in which the composer expresses some particular accidental mood or humor. The form may be handled freely, in the style of a fantasia, or strictly according to rule. The pianoforte caprices of A. B. Muller are fine examples of the latter class.

What is a potpourri?

An arrangement of different and generally well known melodies, for one or more instruments. Many modern fantasias are really nothing but potpourris of this kind.

What is an opera?

A dramatic lyric play, in which poetry, music, painting, and acting united endeavor to excite lively interest and illusion by means of their lifelike presentation of an exciting action. All these means must work together in order to move the heart and strengthen the impression made on the mind and senses.

What special musical forms does the opera include?

The recitative, arioso, cavatina, aria, arietta, duo, terzetto, etc., the ensemble (concerted) pieces, the finale, choruses.

What is an oratorio?

A sacred drama, the words of which are taken from the Bible, or versified from a Biblical subject. It is not intended for dramatic representation, but is calculated for performance by singers and an orchestra. Its form resembles that of the grand opera on the whole, but its style is naturally more serious and churchlike.

What is a hymn?

A religious choral composition, sometimes interspersed with solo movements.

What is a motet?

A church song, generally composed to a short text, Bible verses, etc., containing one especial musical thought, amid which other voices weave a varied contrapuntal web. Between the different strophes, movements appear in the form of the fugue or canon.

What is a mass or missa?

A musical composition set and sung to the words of the principal Catholic service, such as the Kyrie, the Gloria, etc.

**What is a requiem ?**

A mass for the dead (missia pro defunctis).

**What is a cantata ?**

A composition consisting of arias, duets, and choruses arranged according to the incidents of the poem, interspersed with recitatives, which, though resembling the musical drama in its plan form, is intended to be performed without scenic assistance.

**What is a serenade ?**

Music intended to be performed in the evening, under the windows of some person who is to be entertained. Many instrumental compositions are thus named which, without being intended for this particular use, are of a soft and pleasing character.

**What is a nocturne or nocturno ?**

The same thing as a serenade.

---

## SECTION V

### RELATIONSHIP OF THE KEYS, OR MODULATION

**What is meant by related keys ?**

Keys that have several tones in common with each other, C and g major, for example, are keys very nearly related to each other, for g major contains only one tone not to be found in c, namely, f sharp instead of f. D major is also related to c, but not so nearly as g, for it has two tones foreign to c, namely, f sharp and c sharp.

**What are these nearer or more distant relationships styled?**

Degree of relationship.

**F major and g major each differ from c major in one tone alone. What is the difference in their relationship?**

There is none. G major and f major stand related to c major in the same degree.

**How may we easily recognize the different degrees of relationship of the major keys to each other?**

According to the regular succession of keys, by starting from any tone, and then taking its fifth above and its fifth below. Thus:

| ♭ | ♭ | ♭ | ♭ | ♭ | ♭ | ♭ | | ♯ | ♯ | ♯ | ♯ | ♯ | ♯ | ♯ |
|---|---|---|---|---|---|---|---|---|---|---|---|---|---|---|
| 7 | 6 | 5 | 4 | 3 | 2 | 1 | | 1 | 2 | 3 | 4 | 5 | 6 | 7 |
| C♭ | G♭ | D♭ | A♭ | E♭ | B♭ | F | C | G | D | A | E | B | F♯ | C♯ |

If we wish to know what major keys are most nearly related to C, the fifth above and the fifth below give us the key notes, that is, G and F. The keys standing in the second degree of relationship to C are D and B flat major.

**What keys stand in the first and second degree of relationship to B flat major?**

In the first degree, F and E flat; in the second, C and A flat.

**How shall we recognize these degrees of relationship between the minor keys?**

By the same succession of ascending or descending fifths from the key note. We find the upper fifth from a minor, namely, E minor, and its under fifth D minor, stand in the first degree of relationship to it. In this way the different degrees of relationship among the minor scales may also be easily calculated.

**Are there other degrees of relationship?**

Yes; two parallel keys, for instance, C major and A minor, stand in the first degree of relationship to each other, and the major and minor keys placed on the same tone, C major and C minor, for example, also stand in the same degree of relationship. Thus every major and minor key has four other keys related to it in the first degree, two major and two minor

```
   G
   |
c—C—a
   |
   F
```

The key in the center is the accepted principal major key; the large letters standing above and below are the next related major keys, and the small letters at the sides are the most nearly related minor keys. If we take D as the starting point, we arrive at the relationship below:

```
   A
   |
d—D—b
   |
   G
```

And here, starting from a minor key are the nearest degrees of relationship:

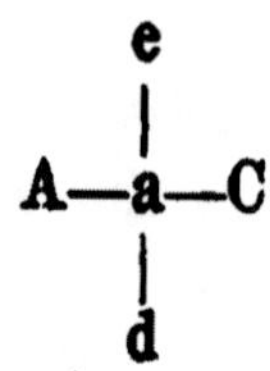


**How shall we find the relationship of the second degree from a major key?**

By seeking out the four nearest related keys to each of the four nearest related keys of the key we first started from. Thus we know that G and F major, a and c minor, are the nearest related keys to c major. Now if we take G major from among these and render it the central point of a new relationship of the first degree, we find its result in the following figure:

*1st figure*

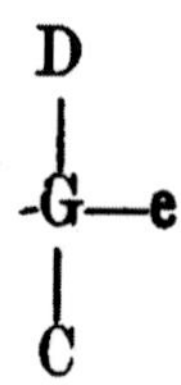


If we take F major as a central point we find:

*2d figure*

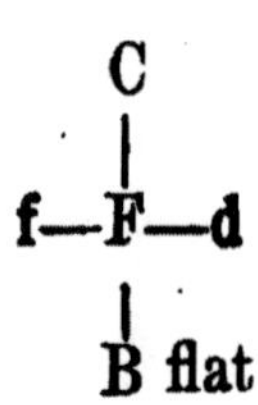

a minor will give us a third figure,

*3d figure*

```
     e
     |
C—a—A
     |
     d
```

and lastly, c minor results, thus:

*4th figure*

```
            g
            |
E flat—c—C
            |
            f
```

Now, if we separate from these tables of relationship, first, the starting keys, which are the four most nearly related to c major, we find as related to c major in the second degree,

*First figure*: D major, g minor, e minor; *second figure*: B flat major, d minor, f minor; *third figure*: A major, e minor, d minor; *fourth figure*: E flat major g minor, f minor; d, e, f, and g minor appear twice, however, yet we find remaining, related in the second degree to c major: D, B flat, A and E flat major, g, d, f, and e minor.

**Do the above remarks apply also to the relationships in the second degree of the minor keys?**

They do.

With a minor, we find related in the first degree e and d minors, C and A major.

Related to e minor in the first degree are b and a minors, G and E majors.

To d minor in the first degree we find a and g minors, F and D major.

Related to C major in the first degree we find G and F majors, c and a minors.

To A major in the first degree we have E and D majors, a and f sharp minors.

Now, if we separate those keys which we found in our first plan of the a minor relationship, and also put aside those keys which are repeated in the above list, we shall find b minor, f sharp minor, g minor, c minor, E major, D major, F major, and G major, all related to a minor in the second degree.

These relationships might be pursued into more distant degrees, but the above will be found sufficient for the scholar's purpose.

---

## SECTION VI

### ELEMENTARY TREATISE ON PIANO TECHNIQUE

These can be briefly divided into three, — finger, wrist, and elbow action. It must be remembered that the position and modes of use of the fingers and arms are not so strongly insisted upon for the sake of gracefulness only; experience and anatomical research has proved that by holding the hands in the position which has been adopted, and lifting the fingers from the knuckle joint, the muscular development is easiest attained, and the greatest amount of force obtained with the least exertion.

A good method of acquiring the finger action is to place the hand, palm downward, flat upon a table, then draw each finger backward as far as possible. The five-finger exercises are wholly intended to develop finger action. Scales, legato passages, etc., are played with this action.

*Wrist action* consists of a swinging of the hand from the wrist joint. The fingers are firm, the wrist loose. Place the fore-arm upon a table, then, without any other motion, raise the hand (by the wrist joint) and strike down, holding the fingers fixed in their normal position. Wrist action is generally used in playing chords, staccato passages, octaves, accented notes, etc.

*Elbow action* consists of a swinging of the entire fore-arm from the elbow joint, holding the wrist and fingers motionless. This mode is used in very full chords, strongly accented notes, etc.

Beyond these motions of finger, wrist, and elbow joint, no others are used. The whole apparatus for the mechanical part of piano playing ends at the elbow joints, and use of the back-arm, swaying of the body, or other motions, are entirely to be avoided. There is at no time to be any straining of muscles, or stiffness. By holding all parts of hand and arm flexible, the pupil will be able to play the longest and most forcible passages with far less exertion than an ordinary passage would take if played with stiff joints and strained muscles.

No master disputes the utility of the daily practice of Scales, but many pupils have a great disinclination thereto; and, though it is not to be doubted that every one will practice them to the extent he may be desired, still as that which is done willingly, and with a conviction of it being conducive to improvement, will always be not only more pleasant, but much more satisfactory in its results, than that which is done as a mere task, the author assures all his pupils that more improvement will be made in one month by those who practice them daily, than will be made in six or even twelve months by those who do not.

The greatest performers never discontinue the practice of scales, and the pupil will find that, by them, he gradually becomes conversant with a proper system of fingering for many passages in music, in which otherwise he would be wholly dependent upon his teacher's suggestions. He will also attain a degree of rapidity of execution and clearness of touch which can be obtained in no other way.

The Common, Dominant, and Sub-Dominant arpeggios, of every key, should also be practiced daily, beginning by striking the chords and then the arpeggios. This will serve a double purpose: not only will it aid the pupil in obtaining manual dexterity and a correct system of fingering, but it will greatly facilitate *sight-reading*. The harmonies used in many of the easier musical pieces consist almost entirely of these three chords, while many seemingly brilliant variations are simply a succession of these arpeggios, and can be mastered very readily by the scholar who practices them daily. The chords should be played sometimes with wrist and sometimes with elbow action. Five-finger exercises are also indispensable to the pupil. A daily practice of these will teach the player how to give the maximum of sound with the minimum of exertion. They are to the pianist what dumb-bells or Indian-clubs are to the athlete. The best of these exercises are those written by Schmidt, Herz, or Czerny. It is to be suggested, however, that the pupil should not play them always in the key in which they are written, but transpose them both up and down the key board, as this will exercise the memory in the various keys, and also *saves the pianoforte*, for nothing wears out a piano so much as five-finger exercises played constantly on the same keys.

These three exercises (scales, arpeggios, and five-finger) are the most necessary daily ones to form the pupil. We would also suggest that it is an excellent plan for the pupil, before playing any piece, to play the scale, chords, and arpeggios of the key in which it is written. This will at once concentrate the mind upon that key, and accustom the fingers to the notes and method of fingering about to be used.

It is scarcely necessary to remark that practice, to be efficient, must be upon a good principle. Practice upon a bad principle, or, what is more common, without any principle at all, will but confirm error, and render it more difficult to conquer. It is, therefore, essential to prevent any bad habit from being acquired; and the very first time a child puts its fingers on the keys, it should be taught to do so in a proper manner. This opinion is much at variance with common practice, which is, to let a child learn *any way* at first, and, when it has contracted all sorts of bad habits, to give it a good master, who has not only to teach, but also to unteach, if, indeed, that can ever be done. A child's learning anything may be compared to the winding of a skein of thread, which, if it have never been tangled may be easily, though perhaps in some instances slowly, wound; but if it be tangled, not only will the trouble be increased tenfold, but the chances are that it will be broken in many places, and consequently never perfect. Some pupils have naturally, that is to say, without any instruction as to how it should be done, a better mode of touching the keys than others, as some persons are naturally more or less graceful in all they do, while others are more or less awkward; but it is not sufficient that anything be well done, it must be done well on principle. Those who have what may be termed a natural good touch, will have less difficulty to contend with; but they must not be allowed to be ignorant of the principle upon which they do well. It is not, however, in the province of these remarks to give a detailed explanation of the principle upon which different passages should be played;

this can only be properly and progressively done by a good instructor.

One thing cannot be too strongly impressed on the mind of the pupil, which is the necessity of patience and perseverance in thoroughly understanding and playing correctly, though perhaps not fluently, the early exercises, as upon these will depend all the future progress. If there be but two notes to be played, still those two notes must be well done, and it is not sufficient that the pupil be able to do them well once or twice, but he must practice doing so; and the rule for going forward must never be when anything has been played a certain number of times, or when it is merely correct, but when, by repetition, it has become habitual to do it well. As an incitement to perseverance, it may be remarked, that those who understand and do play even two notes well, may soon, with the same application, play four, and so on; whereas those who pass over the first two notes, or anything else, without being thoroughly understood, and sufficiently practiced, will never make any satisfactory progress.

For the sake of giving precise directions, it has been assumed that every pupil should practice TWO HOURS A DAY; and it may with truth be said, that those who expect to make any efficient progress should do this at the least. Those who adhere strictly to the directions for the two hours may, it is conceived, from the habits acquired thereby, be safely left to their own discretion for any additional time.

## Practice in General.

Fixed hours should be appointed for practice. It is not enough to say that a pupil should practice two or more hours a day, but the time for so doing should be fixed; every day's experience shows that whatever is left to be done at an uncertain time is frequently left undone, or at best done but imperfectly. Finger exercises should sometimes be played apart from the other studies. Let the scholar, whenever he has ten or fifteen minutes of leisure, seat himself at the piano and play these until quite tired, then rest awhile, and resume again.

The first portion of every hour's practice should be devoted to Exercises or Scales.

Practicing a passage, exercise, or scale does not mean playing it through once, twice, or thrice, but a careful repetition of it twenty or thirty times successively; and the practice of the same should be resumed daily, till it be executed with correctness and precision, and with as much fluency as the progress of the pupil will admit.

The degree of rapidity with which anything is played may be conceded to the age or ability of the pupil; but respecting the principle upon which it is played, there must be no compromise. A pupil, therefore, must not conclude anything to be sufficiently practiced until

Not one wrong key is struck;
Not one wrong finger used;

Not one finger down when it ought to be up, or up when it ought to be down;

The hand held in a proper position throughout;

The piece or passage played in proportion, and without looking at the fingers.

Nothing which fails in any of these particulars can be termed correctly done.

## Rules to be Observed at Practice.

### 1. *Never pass a mistake.*

Never pass over a mistake, but whenever a wrong key is struck, a wrong finger used, if a finger be down or up when it ought to be otherwise, or if the passage be not played in proportion, recommence the passage, and continue to do so till it be done correctly. Passing on, intending to rectify the mistake at another time, will only serve to confirm the error, and render it ultimately more difficult to conquer.

### 2. *Practice slowly at first.*

Avoiding mistakes is better than having them to rectify. Practice, therefore, slowly at first, and when the passage is done correctly, increase the rapidity to the desired degree. It is certain that that which cannot be done correctly slow, will not be correct when done fast. The rapidity may render the incorrectness less observable, but it will not be the less bad.

3. *Ascertain the nature of the difficulty.*

When any passage is found to be difficult, the first point is to ascertain exactly where, and in *what particular*, the error or the difficulty consists. Suppose, for instance, in a passage of twenty notes the difficulty lies in the execution of two or three notes only; in that case, practice those two or three notes till they be done with readiness, and then practice the whole passage.

4. *Practice with each hand separately.*

It may be sometimes advisable to practice a passage with each hand separately. It may be relied on, that if a passage be not played correctly with one hand at a time, it will not be well done with both hands together.

5. *Select passages for practice.*

As all parts of a piece will not require the same degree of practice, select those parts in which there is any difficulty, and practice them. Much time is saved by this method. For example, suppose, in a page of forty bars, there are two which will require practising fifty times, or more, to do correctly; it is obvious that it will be less trouble, and take less time, to practice the two bars fifty times, than the whole page fifty times; besides which, any difficulty will be much sooner surmounted by being played fifty times successively, than if it be played the same number of times, with forty or fifty bars intervening between each repetition.

6. *Practice in small portions.*

When a piece contains no decided comparatively difficult passage requiring to be practiced as above, still it is desirable to practice it in small portions, rather than straight through from the beginning to the end. For instance, suppose two pages containing eighty bars are to be practiced; the pupil will be much more familiarized with the piece by playing portions of eight or sixteen bars, as may be convenient, each twenty times, than if he played the whole eighty bars straight through twenty times.

7. *Caution required in selecting passages.*

In selecting passages for practice, it is desirable not to begin or end always at the same place, unless it be a completely detached passage; otherwise a habit of hesitating or stopping at a particular place will be contracted, which it may be afterwards difficult to overcome.

8. *Extend and reverse passages.*

It is frequently useful to lengthen or extend a passage to a greater compass than may be required in the piece, or, in fact, to make an exercise of it. For example, if an arpeggio extending two octaves require practice, it will be good policy to practice it to the extent of three or four octaves.

It is also desirable, when the passage will admit of it, to practice both ascending and descending, although only one way may be required in the piece.

9. *Repeat correctly six successive times at least.*

No passage that has been badly played should be considered as sufficiently practiced when done once or twice right; SIX SUCCESSIVE times, without error, is the least that can he depended on.

If, on resuming the practice of the same on another occasion, it should be incorrect (as will frequently be the case), it should be practiced till it be done TWELVE SUCCESSIVE times without error, and so on till it can be, with certainty, played correctly.

10. *Practice piece as a whole.*

After practising in detail as above described, the piece must be carefully practiced as a whole from beginning to end. If, in doing this, any mistake should occur, the best remedy is to recommence the whole page or two (nothing fixes the attention as much as this), and continue to do so until

Not one wrong key be struck;

Not one wrong finger used;

Not one finger be down or up when it ought to be otherwise, and until the whole be played through in proportion.

11. *After correctness, practice for fluency.*

Practice, besides being necessary for insuring correctness in any piece or passage, is afterwards requisite for the purpose of gaining more fluency or more finish in the manner of executing it.

### 12. *Practice till perfect.*

Lastly, it may not be amiss to remark that although it is desirable, both by diligence and method, to accomplish as much as possible in the shortest time, still a pupil should remember that, when any piece is played, nobody inquires how often it has been practiced, or how long the performer has been learning it—the only point is, whether it be well or ill done. No stated number of times can, therefore, be fixed upon; but A PIECE SHOULD BE PRACTISED TILL IT BE PERFECT.

Let the scholar remember that the teacher cannot, at every lesson, hear the most indispensable of all — the *Daily Exercises and Scales.* Therefore in this department the scholar becomes, in a slight degree, his own teacher. Upon the faithfulness with which he performs this task, his entire future progress depends.

## Position of the Hand and Arm.

The hand and forearm should be in a straight line from the elbow to the middle joint of the second finger, keeping the wrist neither raised nor depressed. The fingers are to be kept moderately bent and apart (directing particular attention to the second and third fingers, which are more apt to be too close together than the others), so that one finger may be over the center of each key; and the thumb must always be kept over a key. It is of the highest importance to attend to the keeping of each finger over the center of a key, for many persons, notwithstanding they may encompass five keys from the thumb to the little finger, by keeping the other fingers at unequal distances, play indistinctly. For example, supposing the right thumb to play C, in stead of striking F distinctly with the third finger, they strike both E and F with the third finger. Errors of this sort are not at all uncommon, particularly in arpeggio passages, and should be guarded against from the first, by acquiring a habit of keeping each finger over the center of a key.

### Manner of Touching the Keys, or Putting down or Raising the Fingers.

This is a point not generally sufficiently attended to, but it is one of the greatest importance, and should be thoroughly understood and put in practice at first, for the want of a proper manner of putting down and raising the fingers throws great additional difficulty into the execution of every thing that is played, and not only adds difficulty, but gives a bad effect, however perfect the performance may be in all other respects. If the attention be strictly directed to this at first, the proper manner of putting down and raising the fingers will become a *habit* and will cause no trouble afterward; whereas, if this be neglected at first, and the pupil be allowed to practice upon a bad or upon no fixed principle, bad habits will be acquired, and become more or less confirmed, in proportion to the degree of practice, and which, if ever they be overcome, must be at the expense of much labor and time. It is, therefore, essential to prevent any bad habits being contracted.

The rule is simply to hold the finger down on one key till the next is down, but NOT LONGER; or as it may be otherwise expressed:

Two keys which are to be played successively must not be held down together, neither must one be raised till the other is down. In order to direct the attention particularly to this point, it may be as well to remark, that if the finger be held down too long after the following key is struck, it may be so in a greater or lesser degree. For instance, suppose C D are to be played successively, C may be held during the whole, or half, or a quarter of the time after D is down, either of which is wrong, though not equally so. It is not unusual with those who have a bad touch, when five successive keys are played, to find the whole five down at once; so that the first is down four times longer than it ought to be, and the others proportionably so.

It may be remarked, that those who hold the fingers down too much in some places, generally raise them too soon in others. Raising the finger from one key *before* the next is down must equally, as a general rule, be guarded against, as it gives a broken and disjointed effect.

Let it not, however, be conceived that either holding one key down after the next is struck, or taking up before the next be down, is wrong, if marked to be so played. What is intended to be impressed on the mind of the pupil is, that the general rule must be to

Hold one key till the next is down, but NOT LONGER.

And no exercise, passage, or lesson should be played in which this cannot be strictly attended to, until a perfect habit of playing upon this principle is acquired; after which the exceptions, such as raising the fingers at the rests, repeated notes, and those marked to be played staccato, etc., must be learned.

## Preliminary Exercises.

It is important, when striking a key with one finger, to do so without moving the others. To acquire the power of doing this, exercises in which some fingers are held firmly down while the others are moving must be practised. These exercises are termed "preliminary," because they are to be practiced before, and because they differ in principle from all others in this respect, viz., that for the purpose of acquiring for each finger a free action, independent of the others, those fingers which are not employed in playing are to be held down; whereas the general rule in all other exercises is to hold none down but what are actually employed in playing.

The daily practice of these, for a short time previous to other exercises, will always be highly beneficial.

## Looking at the Fingers.

It is essential that the pupil should acquire the power of playing without looking at the fingers. To accomplish this, a little time should occasionally be devoted to this object exclusively.

It must be obvious that the object of all exercises for this purpose will be defeated, if they be played till the pupil remember them; therefore, the same must never be played twice in one day.

Besides those which are expressly intended (by directing the attention for the time being to that object solely) to teach the pupil to play without looking at the fingers, it must be borne in mind that all the other exercises should be played at first, and afterwards practised till they can be executed without once looking at the fingers after first placing the hand.

### The Practice of Exercises.

The greatest difficulties arise from a want of attention to the position of the hand, and the manner of putting down as well as taking up the fingers at the proper places. The attention of the pupil must, therefore, be directed to these points in the practice of exercises until it becomes habitual both to hold the hands well, and touch the keys in a proper manner. Exercises are classed for different purposes, such as the practice of single notes, double notes, arpeggios, etc., and, as passages similar to all exercises will be found in lessons, they will, after being practiced and mastered as exercises, not appear as difficulties when they occur.

## ORDER OF LEARNING AND PRACTISING THE SCALES.

When the pupil is sufficiently advanced, the Scales should be learned and practised daily.

On Mondays, or any fixed day of the week, learn one Major Scale, taken in regular order, and its relative Minor, and practice the same six times or more every day during the week; but, if at the week's end they are not done correctly, and with as much fluency as may be desired, the same must be practised for a week or as many weeks more as may be requisite, before proceeding to the next.

The Scales should be practised in several different ways.

## FIRST MODE OF GOING THROUGH THE SCALES.

Practice with each hand separately, ascending and descending six or more times without intermission.

It may not be useless to remark that, in whichever mode they be practised, the following points must be attended to:

The hand must be held in a proper position throughout.

As one finger goes down, the former must be raised, so that always one, and only one key be down at a time.

In passing the thumb under the fingers, or fingers over the thumb, great care must be taken to do so with as little motion of the hand as possible.

When this is thoroughly, though perhaps slowly accomplished, the pupil may proceed upon the same principle to the scale next in succession, until all have been gone through with.

When all the scales have been practised through in this manner, it will, most probably, be desirable to recommence, and go through the same course again, before proceeding to the next mode.

### Second Mode of going through the Scales.

Practice with both hands together, ascending and descending eight or more times successively. The same directions as to position of the hand, correctness, and repetition, if necessary, of the same scales, must be attended to in this and succeeding modes, as are recommended in the first mode of practising the scales; also, the repetition of the whole course, if necessary.

### Third Mode of going through the Scales.

Instead of ascending and descending as before, practice each scale six or more times, ascending only, and then as many times descending only, with each hand separately.

Practice progressively with increasing rapidity.

### Fourth Mode of going through the Scales.

Practice each scale eight times, or more, ascending only, with both hands together.

Practice progressively with increased rapidity.

## Fifth Mode of going through the Scales.

Practice each scale in thirds, eight times or more.

To play a scale in thirds, begin with the *right hand* on the *third* of the scale, with the finger that would have been upon it had the scale been commenced with the key note, playing at the same time with the left hand in the usual manner.

## Sixth Mode of going through the Scales.

Practice each scale in sixths, eight times or more.

To play a scale in sixths, begin with the *left hand* on the *third* of the scale, (viz., a sixth below the right hand), with the finger that would have been upon it had the scale been commenced with the key note, playing at the same time with the right hand in the usual manner.

## The Practice of Old Lessons.

It is desirable to keep up the practice of the old lessons, but it is presumed that a little time will suffice for that purpose, if they have been properly learned; therefore, at the SECOND HOUR'S PRACTICE, on Tuesdays, Thursdays, and Saturdays, practice an old lesson; if it be done properly, proceed to another; but if not, resume the practice of the same on the appointed days, till it be perfect.

## Playing on the Piano

**From Marx's Musical Instructions.**

After singing, the command of the pianoforte is our most essential qualification, and among us is so considered. The piano is the only instrument, excepting the scarcely accessible organ, on which melody and harmony, and the rich web of combined and simultaneous voices or parts, can be produced with accuracy and almost unlimited magnificence of effect. It is also highly adapted to accompanying song, and to conducting. From these advantages it has happened, that for this single instrument more masterpieces have been written since the time of Sebastian Bach, up to Beethoven, than for all other instruments put together. Most songs have been composed with accompaniment for that instrument — organ parts can be transferred without any change — and whatever quartette or orchestral music found favor with the public, was immediately presented to piano-forte players in the form of arrangements. Therefore, no branch of practice can promise so rich a harvest as piano playing; and it must be acknowledged that, without so abundant a field, any extended acquaintance with our musical literature would be scarcely possible to the world in general. To the composer this instrument is nearly indispensable, partly because no other is so appropriate, both for exercising and exciting his own imagination, and for proving the effect of many part compositions. It is equally important to the conductor and singing master. Even its defects are advantages to musical education, and particularly to the composer. The piano-forte is generally inferior to the bowed and wind instruments in inward feeling and power of *tone* or quality of sounds, in the power of sustaining a *tone*, in equality of force, in crescendo or in diminuendo, in melting two or more *tones* into each other, and in gliding imperceptibly from the one to the other, all which so admirably succeeds on bowed instruments. The piano does not fully satisfy the ear: its performance, compared to that of bowed and wind instruments, is in a manner colorless; and its effect, in comparison with the resplendence of an orchestra, is as a drawing to a painting. But exactly on this account the piano moves more powerfully the creative faculty of both player and hearer; for it requires their assistance to complete and color, to give full significance to that which is but spiritually indicated. Thus imagination fosters the new idea, and penetrates therewith to our hearts; while other instruments immediately seize, and move, and satisfy the senses, and by their means attack the feelings, more powerfully, perhaps in a sensual direction; but not so fruitfully in the soul. This is probably the chief reason why the piano has become the especial instrument for spiritual musical education, and particularly for composition; since other instruments easily overcome their votaries, whom they seduce into their own instrumental peculiarities, and create a one-sided mannerism in their productions.

For the earliest instruction, also, the piano has the advantage (good tuning being supposed) of presenting to the pupil correct *tones*, and a clear insight into the tonal system of the keyboard.

But just from this point arises the important quality of the instrument, which may be perilous to all the real advantages desired from it, unless it be sedulously con-tracted; and this, we must confess, is at present but little thought of, nay, indeed that dangerous quality is speculated on, and an entire false system of education is built on it for outward show, through whose apparent advantages even the true artistic education is represented in a false light, as ignorant and baleful. Since the piano-forte has its fixed *tone* provided, it is easier to play upon this instrument than upon any other, without any internal feeling of correctness of *tone*, or even without hearing, and to arrive at a certain degree of mechanical dexterity. How often do we meet ready piano players, who, from want of a cultivated feeling of *tone*, are incapable of singing a correct succession of *tones* or of imagining it, who have no clear notion of what they are playing, nay, in reality hear nothing correctly! How many bravura players might one name, to whom the artistic meaning of a simple movement remains a sealed book, and who, therefore, perform the greatest and the least compositions with assumption and vanity indeed, but without inward participation, without awakening joy in themselves or in their audience, but merely a fruitless astonishment at their technical clearness. And how deep has this possession of art into dead mechanism penetrated artistic life! Whoever has an opportunity of observing many students of music and their teachers, cannot conceal from himself that at present, particularly in large towns devoted to vanity and fashion, the greater part of the piano-forte students are in this manner led astray; and that a great part of the teachers are themselves ignorant of the right path, or otherwise have not the courage to oppose the stream of fashion, or the allurements of example and personal advantage

If, however, satisfactory instruction is not to be expected from all masters, nor every student is to hope for the choice of a good master, there remains still a tolerably sure method of guarding against this widespread evil. It consists in rigidly examining the work, which is exacted from the pupil himself, and his parents or preceptor insisting absolutely that the teacher shall furnish really profitable work; or, if that cannot be secured with certainty, in seeking immediately another teacher more trustworthy to his art.

We have already said that the pianoforte possesses an extremely voluminous literature, partly written expressly for it, and partly adaptations from other works foreign to it. What can be more natural or more enlightening than to make these works the chief means of instruction; their complete possession being one of the objects of pursuit?

For this end, technical readiness, finger exercises and studies are required. But these are manifestly, only means to an end; and as certainly as their use ought not to be delayed, so certainly also ought they to be set aside when the required dexterity has been gained, and the principal difficulties overcome; or else from a want of methodical arrangement, exercises may be prolonged without end. We cannot conceal from ourselves that in these latter times this error has been stretched to excess, and has overwhelmed us with countless studies, etc. Every respectable teacher, every distinguished amateur, considers himself bound to present the world with some dozens of studies, from which few particular artistic forms of fingering are to be acquired. And since the composition of a well-sounding study exacts nothing but the occurrence of an idea to be worked in the ordinary routine of composition; since, moreover, a little burst of enthusiasm is highly thought of in these matters, and, further, since the brilliant playing of the author, or the reputation of his master renders him tolerably sure of his public, we can never tell when this composition and spread of studies will come to an end; neither, indeed, can we imagine how the pupil shall find time to labor through the most respectable of them only to say nothing of the real works of art themselves for whose sake alone the whole drudgery has been endured.

Let the non-musical enquirer consider the foregoing as a token of good and bad instruction in the question before us.

Sebastian Bach and Handel, Joseph Haydn, Mozart

and Beethoven: these are the artists to whom we owe the greatest and most numerous works of art for the pianoforte. Among these, Bach and Beethoven stand forward, the one in elder, and the other in our times, as those who have reached the highest eminence. After them Emanuel Bach, Clementi, Dussek, Karl Maria, Von Weber, Hummel, and many more may be named. We abstain from giving a more numerous list, particularly of those still living, as it is not the province of this work to pass judgment upon individuals. Upon the highest, the vast preponderance in estimation of the five first named artists, there is not the slightest question among those who have the least tincture of art. The one may indeed be compared with the other, but the pre-eminence of all is unquestionable.

We can, therefore, declare as a condition for good pianoforte teaching, that the works of those five eminent men shall be considered as the distinguished and governing lessons in the instruction. Whatever finger exercises, hand lessons, or secondary work a teacher may find necessary for his pupil, must be left to his decision, as it cannot be estimated. But the teacher who does not conduct his pupil into the study of the five great masters as soon as it can be done with any precision, and the time of the lesson permits it, and does not make them the chief object and goal of instruction, such a teacher, we may say it without hesitation, is not able to give a true artistic education, however clever and careful he may be in other parts of his duty.

Teachers who keep their pupils to fashionable dances and such trifles, to arrangements from favorite operas, etc., are altogether unworthy of the confidence of those who seek for genuine education in art. Therefore, no teacher ought to be chosen without the previous knowledge of his method of instruction.

Pianoforte learning may begin very early, as the seventh or eighth year, or even earlier, even before the hand can span the octave. There is, moreover, a sufficiency of excellent works of Haydn and Mozart, well adapted to the sensibilities of that tender age, if the teacher be but capable of choosing them.

## Music and Children.

(By Dr. A. B. Marx).

Let every mother, who has a perception of the charms of music and of its civilizing influence, weigh well the importance of the early education of the senses. Her simple song, in which perhaps, the infant voice is blended, is the most natural, and often the most fruitful lesson. A march of the most simple melody, and merely drum rhythm, which the boy and his father perform together round about in their apartment, inspires more delight and feeling of measure than many a half-year's instruction. If by great good fortune the tender ear of childhood should be indulged with the delicious enchantment of an opera, the few enraptured hours thus spent may cast a broad and glowing beam of sunshine to the latest days at life. For such an initiation we could wish every child to enjoy the dear old, but ever fresh and young *Bauberflote*, that child's fairy play, which Mozart has immortalized with the power of prolonging and reproducing during all lives, the earliest and most innocent blossoms of youthful delight. In this play, congenial childhood enters with the sweetest self-devotion into the wondrous and inconceivable passions of maturer age, and is carried away at last to the perception of the truth, to the dreadful dagger; but with such guileless purity, such forgetfulness of self, that the star-flaming queen can scarcely be reproached when she rises delicately and without effort in melting harmonies from the midst of her sufferings. On the other hand, we would withhold from the young sensations, the old and revised operas of mere show and exaggerated effect; and more especially those prosaic representations of ordinary life, in which the music sinks with its subject into mere triviality and nothingness. In like manner we would spare our young pupils the affiiction of chamber or social music, which in general they do not understand, and lastly, we recommend moderation in quantity. The first opera once, the full organ in the church when empty; seldom war-like music, and still more rarely, a concert.

These are important moments in the young and impressible existence, and must be of extraordinary occurrences. Moreover, we would petition for the liberty for all children to play freely after their own fashion, on the piano-forte; to invent and search and lose themselves as they please, so long as they do not injure the instrument. This *ad libitum* playing is mostly prohibited, particularly if the days of instruction have begun. The child is told to employ itself more usefully in finger exercises or written compositions. But how shall the individual musical feelings, or the yet feeble inventive imaginings be fostered and educated to self-power and truthfulness, if the only and at this age, indispensable means of cultivation be withheld? We are delighted to hear of the infant Mozart, who in the third year of his short life, sought to arrange sounds in musical compositions; and at the same time, we forbid the like practice to our own children, or disturb their often burning dreams of harmony with our short-sighted and self-sufficient wordly prudence.